W9-CKH-395

Charles Fort

Prophet of the Unexplained

CHARLES FORT

Prophet of the Unexplained

by Damon Knight

Doubleday & Company, Inc., Garden City, New York

1970

I wish to express my thanks to all those who have helped with this book, beginning with Mrs. Betty A. Prashker of Doubleday, who suggested it, and her former assistant Barbara Bikle, whose helpfulness was extraordinary. Aaron Sussman and Mrs. Tiffany Thayer made available a mass of unpublished Fort manuscripts and correspondence; Sussman gave me his own recollections of Charles and Anna Fort. Mrs. Neda M. Westlake, Curator of the Rare Book Division of the University of Pennsylvania Library, and Robert W. Hill, Keeper of Manuscripts at the New York Public Library, made available the Fort material in their collections. Miriam Allen deFord and Edmond Hamilton contributed clippings and correspondence. Mrs. Raymond Fort and her granddaughter, Mrs. Alson J. Spain, furnished family recollections, photographs and correspondence; Faber Birren, Robert Barbour Johnson and Eric Frank Russell gave me their reminiscences of Tiffany Thayer and the Fortean Society. Vincent H. Gaddis lent me his complete file of *The Fortean Society Magazine* and *Doubt*, and Stephen R. Sanderson lent me a copy of *The Outcast Manufacturers*. John R. Pierce and C. L. Mallows of the Bell Telephone Laboratories performed a computer analysis of Fort's data. Richard C. LaBarba, James V. McConnell, Robert S. Richardson, Mrs. Robert Silverberg and Immanuel Velikovsky gave me technical information and many useful suggestions. Robert E. Fisher, George Alec Effinger, Richard S. Buck, Charles Platt and Leslie Shepard aided with research. Twila Decker and Mrs. Patricia Phillips typed the manuscript—and retyped, and retyped it.

Library of Congress Catalog Card Number 70–111340

Printed in the United States of America
First Edition

A Charles Fort Sampler

I believe nothing of my own that I have ever written. I cannot accept that the products of minds are subject-matter for beliefs.

Throw-backs, translated to this earth, would not, unless intensely atavistic, take to what we regard as vices, but to what their own far-advanced people regard as perhaps unmentionable, or anyway, unprintable, degradations. They would join our churches, and wallow in pews. They'd lose all sense of decency and become college professors. Let a fall start, and the decline is swift. They'd end up as members of Congress.

Witchcraft always has a hard time, until it becomes established and changes its name.

I do not know how to find out anything new without being offensive.

I cannot say that truth is stranger than fiction, because I have never had acquaintance with either.

Every science is a mutilated octopus. If its tentacles were not clipped to stumps, it would feel its way into disturbing contacts.

I think we're property.

If the gods send worms, that would be kind, if we were robins.

Mineral specimens now in museums—calcites that are piles of petals—or that long ago were the rough notes of a rose.

—ships from other worlds that have been seen by millions of the inhabitants of this earth, exploring, night after night, in the sky of France, England, New England, and Canada—

I go on with my yarns. I no more believe them than I believe that twice two are four.

If our existence is an organism, in which all phenomena are continuous, dreams cannot be utterly different, in the view of continuity, from occurrences that are said to be real.

I conceive of nothing, in religion, science, or philosophy, that is more than the proper thing to wear, for a while.

. . . I now have a theory that, of themselves, men never did evolve from lower animals: but that, in early and plastic times, a human being from somewhere else appeared upon this earth, and that many kinds of animals took him for a model, and rudely and grotesquely imitated his appearance, so that, today, though the gorillas of the Congo, and of Chicago, are only caricatures, some of the rest of us are somewhat passable imitations of human beings.

Lost tribes and the nations that have disappeared from the face of this earth—that the skies have reeked with terrestrial civilizations, spreading out in celestial stagnations, where their remains to this day may be. The Mayans—and what became of them? Bones of the Mayans, picked white as frost by space-scavengers, regioned to this day in a sterile luxuriance somewhere, spread upon existence like the pseudo-breath of Death, crystallized on a sky-pane.

The interpretations will be mine, but the data will be for anybody to form his own opinions on.

The unadulterated, whether of food we eat, or the air we breathe, or of idealism, or of villainy, is unfindable. Even adultery is adulterated.

. . . the astronomers are led by a cloud of rubbish by day and a pillar of bosh by night—

Do unto others as you would that others should do unto you, and you may make the litter of their circumstances that you have made of your own. The good Samaritan binds up wounds with poison ivy. If I give anybody a coin, I hand him good and evil, just as truly as I hand him head and tail. Whoever discovered the uses of coal was a benefactor of all mankind, and most damnably something else. Automobiles, and their seemingly indispensable services—but automobiles and crime and a million exasperations. There are persons who think they see clear advantages in the use of a telephone—then the telephone rings.

Contents

Life Everlasting—based on a misprint!
I mused as I drove homeward: take the hint,
And stop investigating my abyss?
But all at once it dawned on me that *this*
Was the real point, the contrapuntal theme;
Just this: not text, but texture; not the dream
But topsy-turvical coincidence,
Not flimsy nonsense, but a web of sense.
Yes! It sufficed that I in life could find
Some kind of link-and-bobolink, some kind
Of correlated pattern in the game,
Plexed artistry, and something of the same
Pleasure in it as they who played it found.

It did not matter who they were. No sound,
No furtive light came from their involute
Abode, but there they were, aloof and mute,
Playing a game of worlds, promoting pawns
To ivory unicorns and ebon fauns;
Kindling a long life here, extinguishing
A short one there; killing a Balkan king;
Causing a chunk of ice formed on a high-
Flying airplane to plummet from the sky
And strike a farmer dead; hiding my keys,
Glasses or pipe. Coordinating these
Events and objects with remote events
And vanished objects. Making ornaments
Of accidents and possibilities.

Stormcoated, I strode in: Sybil, it is
My firm conviction—"Darling, shut the door.
Had a nice trip?" Splendid—but what is more
I have returned convinced that I can grope
My way to some—to some—"Yes, dear?" Faint hope.

Vladimir Nabokov, *Pale Fire,* Canto Three

Introduction

Charles Fort was convinced that there is a great deal going on in our universe which man has not as yet been able to explain. He was, of course, right. Fort amassed reports of events allegedly observed by humans around the world. Fort's books are full of reports of strange phenomena—such as those similar in every way to today's reports of flying saucers but centuries before they were called flying saucers.

Boole gave scientists a powerful tool for attacking problems when the obvious approaches refused to yield informative results. Boole employed *reductio ad absurdum.* He exhausted all the impossibles and thereby isolated a "very probable" answer. Charles Fort, failing to gain the publishers'—and thereby society's—consideration of his positive theories, left world society with a Boolean-like confrontation of illogical events.

Charles Fort as a man of true vision purposefully inverted the equations. By getting the publishers to publish the absurd, he proved his point that the publishers published only the absurd.

A counterpart of Charles Fort, whose work has turned out to be extraordinarily important, was Matthew Fontaine Moray. Thoroughout the ages of men, those going to sea had reported that they had seen sea serpents, many other kinds of monsters, great mile-wide whirlpools, and psycho-perils such as sirens. Matthew Fontaine Moray—a junior officer in the United States Navy before the American Civil War—became a Confederate officer. After the war was over, he went back into the federal service. He said he thought it would be important for humanity to exercise a heretofore unemployed capability.

When ships come in from the high seas through the customs, they all have to register. Moray suggested that the United States should require that all watch-to-watch observational data from the ships' logs be recorded. Everyone who goes to sea knows what must be entered in the log. The men on watch record the weather conditions; the force and direction of the wind; the temperature of the air and the water; the barometric pressure; the condition of the sea; the cloud formations; other ships sighted; their own course and speed, etc.

By doing this, Moray collected so much data from around the world for each of all the days of many years that, aided by large crews of workers, he was able to show the simultaneous conditions around the world and the progressive changes that were taking place and could be correlated.

Gradually it was discovered that there were ocean currents. Gradually it was discovered what the shape and most probable course of storms are. Gradually they discovered the basic patterns of the Northern and Southern Hemispheres' prevailing winds—clockwise in the Northern

Hemisphere and counterclockwise in the Southern Hemisphere—the reverse cycling of the atmosphere and waters around the equator and the beginnings of the awareness of the West to East roaring jet streams.

Matthew Fontaine Moray made available to humanity all the available reports from all around the world. By looking at them, students and seamen began to see what was predictable.

The other instance I'll give is that of a man at Grand Canyon with a moving-picture camera. It was a day when the Grand Canyon was full of mist. The tourists felt frustrated because they couldn't see into the canyon. The man turned on his moving-picture camera and took one frame every minute and then later ran the pictures he had taken of the mist at a rapid rate. To his astonishment, he found that the accelerated picture of that mist in the Grand Canyon showed that it was behaving like coffee in a cup on a railroad train—it was articulating waves. You could see the waves operating. These waves in the seeming reality were moving too slowly for any human eye to see.

Though I cannot remember doing so, I may have met Fort, because, before he died I knew and spent time with his friend, Theodore Dreiser, along with some of the latter's friends present. I knew Fort's especially admiring friend, Tiffany Thayer, who six years after Fort's death made me a life fellow of the Fortean Society which Thayer had founded. My book, *Nine Chains to the Moon,* published in 1938, was the occasion of Thayer's doing so. But in a very real sense—probably the realest—I have met Fort in his writing.

Over a very large period of time, I think that the total data recorded by Charles Fort from around the world may prove of great scientific worth. Above all this, there is something extremely inspiring about Fort's interest in his universe. His interest is very romantic. It isn't written in romantic terms at all, but the man is full of dreams—dreams of significance. Fort was in love with the world that jilted him. Fort, like humanity, was looking for significance in experience. Fort is becoming increasingly popular with the university students who all around the world are looking for significance. Billions of young people are in love with a world whose complexity seems to be trying to jilt them. I don't think their love will be unrequited. They will be interested in Damon Knight's portrait of a man who, with humor and tenderness, tried to show the irreversible evoluting scenario of the universe and suggest that the next installment is always a surprise, the grand theme eternally elusive.

—R. Buckminster Fuller

Chapter One

Three Brothers (1874–1891)

It was told in the New York *World,* July 29, 1908—many petty robberies, in the neighborhood of Lincoln Avenue, Pittsburgh—detectives detailed to catch the thief. Early in the morning of July 26th, a big, black dog sauntered past them. "Good morning!" said the dog. He disappeared in a thin, greenish vapor.

There will be readers who will want to know what I mean by turning down this story, while accepting so many others in this book.

It is because I never write about marvels. The wonderful, or the never-before-heard-of, I leave to whimsical, or radical, fellows. All books written by me are of quite ordinary occurrences.

Wild Talents

He spent twenty-six years of his life collecting reports of unusual happenings—rains of frogs, of blood; disappearances, "phantom bullets," poltergeist phenomena. He ruined his eyesight in library reading rooms, and was almost blind for a year, but recovered and went on.

Ben Hecht said, "I am the first disciple of Charles Fort." *Time* mocked him as "a convinced prophet of footless negation." The novelist Tiffany Thayer, author of *Thirteen Men,* founded the Fortean Society in his honor; Fort said he would not join it, any more than he'd be an Elk. He was loved by those who knew him, including his friend and patron Theodore Dreiser, but he hated company, seldom went out or saw visitors, and would not even have a telephone.

He began his professional career as a humorist, writing stories for magazines about his tenement neighbors in the New York slums. He was as poor as they were. Some of his funniest stories were written when he had pawned everything he owned. Even then, his curiosity drove him to take thousands of notes on all kinds of subjects—on "climate in the Eocene and tricks of shyster lawyers; conventionalism in art and South American revolutions; notes upon drygoods clerks and arrangements of floating magnets; domestic infelicity, tropisms of zoospores, and mutual repulsions of boardinghouse characters." He had twenty-five thousand notes, in pigeonholes that covered a wall; they were not what he wanted, and he destroyed them. He accumulated forty thousand more. Eventually he began to see an unsuspected pattern in them.

Fort's father, an Albany businessman, was an autocratic Victorian. Fort grew up hating intolerance, and found a way of opposing it that had never occurred to anyone else—by championing the data that cannot be explained and are therefore ignored. He called them "the damned": "By the damned, I mean the excluded."

In four books, *The Book of the Damned, New Lands,*

Lo!, and Wild Talents, he assembled more than twelve hundred documented reports of happenings which orthodox science could not explain. His data were like unwanted children deposited on scientists' doorsteps. He never presumed to explain them himself: he merely said, "Here they are." But he speculated about them, sometimes with tongue in cheek. He imagined a stagnant area somewhere above us, a "Super-Sargasso Sea," where things carried up from Earth hang suspended until, disturbed by superstorms, they fall to the surface again—slag, coke, sulfur, little insects, frogs. It seemed no more believable to him, he said, that a world as full of waste and pain as ours is organized for the benefit of human beings, than that a stockyard is organized for the benefit of hogs. He wrote, "I think we're property."

In later years, even after an inheritance had made him financially secure, he lived quietly in small London and New York apartments. He liked home brew and rattrap cheese. He went to the movies with his wife, Anna, nearly every night.

When he died in 1932, he left as his monument a massive collection of inconvenient, frustrating, stubbornly resistant data. And the things he wrote about have gone right on happening.

Albany, the seat of government in New York State, was founded in 1624 by eighteen families of Dutch Walloons, on the site of a trading post and fort built by the United New Netherland Company. Railways converge at Albany; it is served also by steamboats on the Hudson, and by the state barge canal system. The inhabitants call themselves Albanians. They are proud of their colonial history, of the cheerful corruption of their government, and of their fat purses. Albany is not Boston or New York or Philadelphia; it is Albany, and goes its own way.

In the late nineteenth century, one of the leading citizens of Albany was Charles Nelson Fort, the descendant of an old Dutch family,[1] son of Peter V. Fort, a wholesale grocer. Charles's wife Agnes was the daughter of another leading citizen, John Hoy, a dealer in plumbing supplies. Their marriage was happy. Between 1874 and 1878 Agnes Fort bore her husband three sons—Charles Hoy,[2] Raymond, and Clarence. The husband was handsome, the boys healthy, the wife pretty and vivacious.

A few weeks after Clarence's birth, Fort and his young wife attended a ball in the governor's mansion. Those older persons who said it was too soon, and that no good would come of it, were right. Agnes was ill the next day; a few weeks later she died.

There is evidence that Charles Nelson Fort deeply loved his wife, and never recovered from his loss. More than thirty years later, when he was on his deathbed, he had a picture of Agnes hidden under his pillow.[3]

A few months after his wife's death, Charles Nelson Fort bought a new house near the Albany country club. The three boys were installed on the top floor, with swings and a seesaw. Charles was four, Raymond two; Clarence was an infant. Mrs. Lawson, the housekeeper, had charge of them during the day, but as time went on, three active and unprincipled small boys were sometimes more than she could handle. Matters of discipline were dealt with by the boys' father.

Charles Nelson Fort treated his sons with a severity common in Victorian times but almost incredible today. Charles Fort mentions casually that he was beaten with a dog whip, and adds that he objected to the butt end.

In Mrs. Lawson's room one day. She was teaching us our Sunday school lesson; it was about Moses and the rock. They strolled in, brushing their hat, looking into the mirror to see that the necktie was all right, very particular with every detail of their appearance. Then Moses smote the rock. But they flurried us; we could not pronounce "smote." An easy word, but we said "smut." Told to read it over; again we said "smut." More flurried; unable to use our brain; saying "smut" still again, because our lips formed that way and we had no brain. To them, we were showing dogged meanness. They struck us in the face.

"That's smote," They said. "Now do you understand what smote is?" . . .[4]

This quotation is from an unpublished autobiography, *Many Parts,* which Fort wrote in 1901. He kept trying to sell it until 1909, but no one would have it. In this manuscript, only fragments of which survive, Fort speaks of himself as "we." Raymond is "the other kid"; Clarence, "the little kid." Their father is always referred to as "They."

On another occasion, Fort's father struck him in the face. Blood gushed from his nose. ("Toddy's nose bleeds so readily," said Mrs. Lawson.) In a passion of fury, he ran upstairs into the spare bedroom, rubbed his bloody face all over the counterpane, the carpets, the lace curtains, leaving the room as gory as the scene of an ax murder.[5]

The boys were forbidden to speak or make any sound at the dinner table; the sound of their voices offended

Them. Once, says Fort, the restraint was too much for him and he giggled nervously.

> They looked over the newspaper, saying, "Who's that!" The little kid started to tell; he kept quiet. The other kid answered that he had heard nothing. We said, "I did it." Mrs. Lawson would have told anyway; we wanted credit for truthfulness.
>
> "Go upstairs!" We rising slowly, eating pie as we rose. We going up inch by inch; pie going down inch by inch. Couldn't bear to leave that pie. And this was defiance to Them. Jumping from their chair, catching us by the collar, hitting us in the face with their open hand.
>
> We running up the stairs, striking at figures in the wallpaper, butting our head against the bannister, trying to kill ourself, biting our arms, running up and down the hall in frenzy. They went out, and, when the other kids came up, we were leaning over the bannister, letting blood drip into the lower hall to do damage. We knew it was dirty work; had as much sense of decency as a grown person; only, just then we were a little beast.[6]

Kids were wilder in those days, and were accordingly punished more; or else they were punished more, and that made them wild; take your choice.

Mrs. Lawson was a gentle soul. To her, and to the children because they loved her, plants were creatures that could think and feel. One fall afternoon, there were flowerpots and window boxes scattered everywhere. Mrs. Lawson called to the boys, and they helped for all they were worth, digging and transplanting, for Jack Frost was coming. Great excitement when Mrs. Lawson told them Jack Frost was only a mile away. They worked like stevedores, and got all the plants indoors to safety, just as Jack Frost peeked around the church steeple. Only the sunflowers were left behind, and this worried the boys; they dug one up and smuggled it to the top floor to save it too.

Fort liked Sunday school, and felt occasional pangs of religious emotion, though when all who wanted to be Christians were asked to raise their hands, he could never bring himself to raise his. In church he amused himself by shooting spit wads, keeping score: a bald head, fifteen, ears, ten. At home Mrs. Lawson warned against the devil; she called him "the Old Boy," and sometimes drove him away from the window with a broom. Fort learned that every time he told a white lie, a little white mark would appear on one of his fingernails; for a black lie, a canker on the tongue. Conscience often kept him awake, and then he would go downstairs to confess to Mrs. Lawson, "faltering and writhing, but feeling that every word lessened the burden"; then Mrs. Lawson would take him in her arms and sing him to sleep.

By daylight there were fascinating things all around him: grasshoppers on the lawn, big black ants in a hollow pear tree. He exposed himself to darning needles, found it was untrue that they sew up little boys' ears. He caught a wasp, holding it triumphantly by the head so it could not bite, then discovered that it bit with the other end.

He bought birds' wings from a boy at school; he found a store where he could buy, for pennies, dried starfish, sea urchins, shells, sea beans. In his geography book he traced imaginary voyages with a pencil: the South Sea Islands, Madagascar.

Old Peter V. Fort, Charles's grandfather, was a man of little education. In his library at home there were bound sets of the works of Ruskin and Carlyle, bright and new. In the grocery store he had two offices—one where he looked after his interests in real estate and loaned money (usuriously, Fort discovered later), and another, his private office, where he gathered with his cronies and concocted strange drinks. In this office he kept the well-worn books he really liked—histories, biographies, and travel books, including half a dozen about Arctic expeditions. Fort found him there one afternoon reading a heavy book, with a pink drink on one side of him and a yellow drink on the other.

He once asked Fort what he wanted to be when he grew up; Fort answered, "A naturalist." This seemed to puzzle the old man; he went away, probably to consult the dictionary which he kept between a demijohn and a jug. After a while he returned, looking even more puzzled. Science was all well enough as a hobby, but birds and animals were important to a businessman only when they were in cans on a counter.

Fort stopped buying birds' wings; he had made a slingshot and learned to use it. He struck his first victim, a bluebird, and saw it flutter down with as much amazement as if a piece of the sky had fallen.

He cut off the wings, scalps, and tails of his prizes and mounted them on white cards. He grew so expert with the slingshot that he could knock a sparrow off a telegraph wire nearly every time. "Beaks opening helplessly at us; useless wings spread out, feebly beating the ground, we fiercely exulting, knowing nothing of pity, though to end suffering, we would break necks without injuring the skin."

He stalked birds on all-day expeditions in the woods

outside Albany. When he shot a strange bird, he would go home to search through books of natural history for it; next day he would be back to hunt for the bird's mate; he tried to collect male, female, young, and eggs of every species.

Later he got an air gun; and with that air gun in his hands, Fort says, he had no civilized instincts. He saw a fine robin on a lawn. There were people on the piazza, but he jumped the fence, kneeled, aimed. A woman screamed; a gardener started toward him; another woman was imploring him not to shoot.

He killed the robin. He mounted it. It was a little weak about the knees, perhaps, but its chest was thrown out proudly. He kept the insides for dissection. He was dissecting all kinds of creatures now; kept a noose on the cat path under the fence. He mounted skeletons, preserved organs in alcohol.

In partnership with Raymond, he began to sell his specimens. While he sat up late skinning and stuffing them, Raymond would be "traveling"—notifying customers to be on hand next day to see the goods. "We'd sell eighty cents' worth perhaps; forty in cash, twenty sure and the rest in bad debts."[7]

They also dealt in birds' eggs, and sometimes their practices were sharp. They sold grosbeak eggs from sparrows' nests, and counterfeit oriole eggs. If a collector complained, the partners would say, "Baltimore or orchard oriole? Who said it was? It's a Bizzingum Oriole, which is very rare north of Central America. Why don't you study up?"[8] And the collector would go away to boast of his bizzingum egg.

The partners also dealt in stamps, bought from mail-order firms. ". . . for a few cents something from Africa would be sent to us; little square bits of Japan; trifles that seemed a part of Peru. . . ." To get the little capital they needed, they "spoiled" stamped envelopes at the store and took them to the post office for refunds. Sometimes their father wondered where all the envelopes were going; but "both of us knew enough not to spoil envelopes too often; we had the wisdom and self-control that the true criminal has not; so we were never caught."[9]

When Fort was about thirteen, his father married again. The new bride was Blanche Whitney, a member of a prominent Albany family. The first reference to her is on page 82 of *Many Parts;* the previous two pages are missing. "And then our new mother won us as really and truly our new mother by getting scissors and trimming the little kid's hair so that no one else should ever know."

This must have been before the wedding; it appears that the boys had been sent to visit her at home.

> "You collect stamps?" our new mother asked. "If you'll tell me where to get them, we'll go now." And all together we cried where an old collector of stamps lived. And to the old collector we went, trying not to be greedy, making our new mother's admission fee into the family as reasonable as we could. And then walking back with her, thinking it would be very bad manners to leave her in the street, though we very much wanted to get back to the album with our new stamps.
>
> And on our way back, the first thing we said was, "She's all right!" Denouncing all that had lied about her. And we'd defend her; and we'd do everything chivalrous. We all excited. Just what wouldn't we do![10]

It appears from what follows that both the new stepmother and the boys tried hard to get along; but they never quite succeeded.

There is something in human lives that mocks our belief in free will. Looking back, we can see that the boys' futures, instead of being a blur of potentialities as they seemed, were as fixed as if they had been cast in concrete.

Clarence, who worshiped his older brothers and would do anything for them, had no other human allegiance, nor any fear of punishment. He did outrageous things with an air of indifference, almost of inattention. Fort gives us a glimpse of him, playing in the front yard while Mrs. Lawson is supposedly watching through a window. Clarence steps on some plants deliberately; the expected tapping of a thimble on the windowpane does not come, so he knows Mrs. Lawson's attention is elsewhere. He goes to the fence, lures the even smaller next-door kid close to it, then reaches under, "starting to pull his neighbor through a space about big enough for cats. Very little kid screaming; little kid pulling away on a very little leg. Parents crying to him; little kid pulling away without excitement; very little kid coming through with a jerk, most of his clothes scraped off."[11]

Charles was the skeptic, the one who was always asking, "Why?" He did poorly in school, because he could never resist any opportunity to be funny; but at home he read avidly, teaching himself taxonomy, scraps of foreign languages, natural history, mythology, geography.

Raymond, the middle brother, was the calculating one, the good businessman. When the three boys played a trading game of their own invention, it was Raymond who would not bargain; the other two would have to sell at his price, buy when he wanted to sell.

He and Charles were joint owners of a collection of

birds' eggs; Charles, who could not bear to divide ownership with anyone, wanted to buy him out, but had no capital. ("Always wanting something; and not a cent from Them."[12]) Raymond set a stiff price, and let Charles pay it off by doing his work and taking his punishments. A dime off for shoveling snow, while Raymond sat by, getting his ten cents' worth of labor and twenty cents' worth of satisfaction.

Or, at the dinner table, their father says, "Who's making that noise?" Raymond, who is guilty, looks significantly at Charles. Charles, feeling the weariness of slavery, answers, "Me."

"Say 'I.' Go upstairs!"[13]

Charles goes; and Raymond crosses off another dime.

Nevertheless, their loyalty to each other was strong. Charles was growing too big to thrash ("They struck us no more after the time we had forced them almost to the floor"[14]), so a new kind of punishment began. I give this in Fort's words, for fear of being disbelieved if I paraphrase it.

> No longer beating us, but locking us in a little, dark room, giving us bread and water, sentencing us to several days or several weeks of solitude. Three times a day the door would be opened, and bread and water would be thrust into darkness. Three times a day a bundle would come down the air shaft. At the table, the other kids would sit with handkerchiefs on their knees, slipping in things when no one was looking. So well did we take care of one another that when two were serving terms, the free one would be the starved one.
>
> Books coming down the air shaft, and matches

> to light the gas with. We sitting in the little window, writing our name and date on the white wall, adding, "Imprisoned here for doing nothing," which, we believe, is the view of most criminals. It would please us to write these things, feeling that many years later we, then a great, famous man, should like to come back and look at them. Often we'd have this feeling that the great, famous man would like to see relics of his childhood. . . .
>
> We in prison, and They turning the gas fixtures so that we should be in darkness. A monkey wrench coming down the air shaft. Sitting sometimes with the gas burning but oftener in darkness, we a lazy kind of boy but tortured with the awfulness of doing nothing. Then singing to make the time hasten. Melancholy songs, we an unfortunate, little boy, persecuted for doing nothing, crying a little in sympathy with the poor, little boy, who had never done anything wrong. Then singing patriotic songs, half defiantly because of the noise we were making. About "Let freedom ring." Adding, "Freedom don't ring here." Hearing our new mother, under the air shaft, laugh at this. Then we, too, would laugh; for we could never be mean when others were not.[15]

Victorian children were brutally treated at times, ignored at others. Perhaps they had a little more freedom and privacy than we do. With a whole floor to themselves, a common enough thing then, the boys could do pretty much what they pleased; like other Victorians, they were used to providing their own amusements.

In bed at night, Charles and Raymond told installments of an adventure story that had been going on for years. For half an hour or so they might have business matters to discuss; then they'd whistle for Clarence. No matter how long that signal was delayed, it would be followed by the sound of little bare feet on the floor, and they would see Clarence flitting through the beams from the skylight, getting into bed with them to hear the stories.

The two older brothers also played elaborate games with paper soldiers. Each wanted the blue-coated soldiers, but Fort always wound up with the redcoats, because if Raymond could not have the Americans he would not play. They slung book covers at each other's armies, taking prisoner all that they knocked down. They gave them individual names and personalities, awarded them medals for extraordinary achievements, such as landing on their feet when knocked across the room. But Raymond was stern with his soldiers; when they failed to live up to their records, he degraded them, hanged them, burned them at the stake.

> Other times, when They were out, we'd light the gas, and get a remarkably big ironing board from a room used as a storage room. Tobogganing down the stairs, going at fearful speed, knocking all to pieces the baseboard at the bottom. Or having theatrical performances when we were supposed to be fast asleep. Our favorite play was the "Gunpowder Plot." We'd often write a little play patched up from our reading, giving parts for the others to learn. We were King James sitting on his throne, which was a chair on the bed, and the other kid was Guy

> Fawkes, looking very wicked in burnt-cork whiskers. The ignorant, little kid not knowing much about the part he was playing, but thinking he knew, which seems to be enough for any actor.[16]

Even without the beatings and solitary confinement, Fort and his brothers would have had miseries enough—compulsory oatmeal, goose grease, sulfur and molasses. But it is hard to think of them as deprived children. They had a romantic innocence that we have lost; the world was wonderful to them.

Fort hunted for Indian relics. Finding none, he practiced archaeology in reverse—buried whatever he had in his pockets, even pennies, "for someone to find a thousand years later and be pleased with."[17] At home he pried up floorboards and put paper soldiers or marbles under them; he slipped other treasures down cracks between walls and floor, like an alderman burying a time capsule. He put sticks on car tracks, to honor them as heroes for having been run over. He left a book on the roof all winter, "picturing its hardships when the snow was falling, pleased with it in the Spring, all faded, with leaves undulating and cover warped."[18]

With Biff Allen, a school friend, he built a bobsled and an ice boat. "The ice boat would not go through the door, to be sure, and the river was a mile away, and it was not completed until June, but as a specimen of the ship-builder's art it caused us great pride."[19]

Later Biff proposed to Charles and Raymond that they should all run away to Burma and be elephant drivers at eighteen dollars a week. The partners sold their stamps for fifteen dollars; Biff's contribution was a pile of dime novels, which he assured them would be worth its weight in gold during the long evenings around campfires. Biff also suggested that they lay in a good stock of provisions; so every day relays of boys went down to "the store"—always so called, though it was really a warehouse—and came back with cans of sardines, stuffed olives, peaches.

Clarence wanted to go along, but would not plead. He came to them one day when they were in Biff's garret, looking at an enormous stack of canned goods. He handed them a parcel, saying, "It's provisions." Inside was a big pickle, stolen from a corner grocery. "We told him that he was a good, little kid, and we should always remember him when away off in foreign climes. 'Foreign climes' too much for him; making awful faces, trying not to cry."

> Four o'clock. We up and ready to start for India, having said good-bye the evening before to the little kid, who had given up talking of going with us. We went to his room to see him once more. Fast asleep, but all his clothes were on, and he hugged a bundle under one arm. We wavered at this; but India is no place for small boys. So we kissed him good-bye; and the other kid kissed him good-bye.[20]

Biff was not on the corner where they had agreed to meet; he did not turn up until nine, when he told a story of wandering sleepless down to the river, there saving a man from drowning. The adventure was postponed, then forgotten.

In Raymond's opinion, the whole thing had been a scheme of Biff's to help his family lay in provisions for the winter. Fort could hardly believe in such duplicity, but whenever he went through Biff's dining room, there were always pickles on the table. When he played in Biff's yard, he was embarrassed by stumbling over lobster cans. There were soup cans everywhere, and he pretended not to see.

When the partners had turned a profit, they might sit for an hour with a stamp catalogue between them trying to decide how to spend the money; but in the end one would say, "Let's treat Clarence." Once they took him down to the river, but were overwhelmed by responsibility. They made him sit well back from the tide line, then still farther back. When he wanted to hunt for shells, they watched every step he took. He wanted to go in wading. They were horrified, but let him go in up to his knees. Then they had to show him how wonderful they were. Charles swam "at least ten strokes"; Raymond sat down with his head actually underwater. Clarence was impressed. But they never took him to the river again; the strain was too great. Next time they treated him, they took him to the park, and "even there the swings went too high."[21]

In 1889 Clarence was consigned to a correctional institution called Berkshire Farm, in Canaan, New York. We do not know what his crime was. He was ten years old.

> "We are indeed three brothers—" It was too much for the little kid. He leaned against a fence post, and put up his arm. He didn't want us to see him cry.
>
> And it was too much for us, for we were looking at the little kid, with his little arm up.
>
> Our same old madness; some of it because we

were seized upon, some of it to impress the others. Crying that we should kill Them. Butting our head against a post. Knocked flat. Butting and falling in frenzy, trying to kill ourself or whatever the post meant to us. The other kid looked on, disapproving; the little kid stood erect, not a sign of anything at all on his face.

We said no more. Covering the jars with earth; marking the place with pebbles for grave stones. All three sat on the piazza, saying very little. They took the little kid away.

Evening. Going to the dining room. We had been crying all afternoon, and felt that if there were the slightest reference to the little kid we should break down. And we and the other kid paused in the doorway. For we saw something. What the other kid saw was a smaller table; a leaf had been taken out. This was sensible to the other kid; the table had been too large anyway. He went to his chair to eat his supper, which was what he had gone down to do.

What we saw was the meaning of a vacant chair in the leaf that had been taken from the table. Littleness there brought to us littleness that was no longer there. We could not move and we could not speak. Just standing there, the other kid looking at us as if wondering what new flightiness could be the matter with us.

They looked from the newspaper; we had feared that look once.

We said, "Oh!" Just softly, because we were choked and quivering. . . .[22]

That fall Fort entered high school, another new world. He was attracted by one of the teachers, Miss North, "who knew everything that had ever been heard of."

In science class he learned skepticism. The professor demonstrated that in a vacuum a bullet and a feather fall with equal speed (the bullet fell first); that white is a mixture of all colors (he mixed them, produced a brownish gray); that black absorbs more heat than white (he put a black cloth and a white one in the sun on the snow-covered windowsill: the white cloth made a decided impression in the snow, the black one, not a trace).

Fort's grades were so bad that he dared not show them, and had to practice forgery. He barely scraped through the year, with a "condition." When summer came, nevertheless, he was sent to a Y.M.C.A. camp on Lake Champlain. He was so pleased that he became friends with Them again: "No more sullenness, we going down to their room where we had not been in a long time, to play chess, just as we had long before, talking about fishing and hunting, very good friends, everything forgotten and forgiven at last."[23]

For some time he had been keeping a diary, collecting scenes, incidents, characters, as if they were birds and stones. The experience of outdoor life at Lake Champlain moved him profoundly; he wanted to write about his sentiments, but his instinct for humor got the better of him. "Urged to write of darkness and light left behind. Unable to; writing instead of filling a fish with a pound of shot and betting it would weigh more than a larger fish. Having an impression of the way singing made us feel; writing of pouring molasses into Crayley's shoes."[24]

At home nothing had changed. What Fort wanted most was a good suit of black cheviot to wear to school; what he got was a suit of dark brown with faint yellow stripes. It was so tight that it made his legs bulge; the brown dye came off on his hands. After a few weeks he went through the seat of the pants. No one offered to mend them; when he went to the blackboard, he had to walk backward. "Up in our room, looking at thread and needle, but feeling it beneath us to do any sewing. Progressive euchre down stairs; costly prizes; everything always done on a scale that was costly. We upstairs trying to sew rags together. And succeeding very well, we thought. Sitting down. Swish! Worn out cheapness could not keep those big, fat legs in. So we pounded a chair, just as, when a little boy, we had pounded chairs. . . ."[25]

Fort was the class comedian, pretending to hang a hat on an invisible projection of the German professor's bald head. When he made a speech in the auditorium, he left the students in such a state of hilarity that he was not invited to speak again.[26]

He still could not manage to turn his mind to the work that was required. "A teacher would ask some simple question in geometry; there were we silenced as if with a mind darkened. Asking about some perplexing kind of an accusative; we without a sign of intelligence. Teacher asking some question with the answer not in our school book, such as, 'What great author once submitted drawings to Dickens, who rejected them?' Turning instinctively to us, for our hand would be sure to be up, we all eagerness, no lack of intelligence and no mind darkened. Obscure and trivial questions; we with the facts in our storehouse; our hand waving excitedly."[27]

His thoughts turned more and more to writing. Miss North encouraged him, and so did his maternal uncle, John S. Hoy, referred to in *Many Parts* as "Nick."[28]

> Nick was interested in our writings for the literary society, and often asked to see what we had written, showing us where we had labored around and around a point expressible in a few words. Just before school closed, he sent for us. Saying, "How would you like the newspaper business?" We answering, "Oh, all right," by which we meant that nothing could be more attractive for us. . . .
>
> Nick said, "Well, go around to the 'Democrat'; Standish is editor there now, and he will put you on. There won't be much of anything in it for you at first, but it will give you an idea, and some day we may get you down in New York. Just keep your rubbers on, and you'll not slip up."

Fort went to work on the Albany *Democrat,* eager and awkward as a puppy. When he handed in his first assignment, the copy reader gave it back with the remark, "The puzzle editor isn't in just now." Standish advised him to cultivate a large, round hand, "remarking that he had known poor writers to produce legible work in that way." Fort painstakingly recopied his story, making each letter "large as a bean." The story was printed, and he went on to write others. For years after, his handwriting was of two kinds—his own idiosyncratic scrawl, and the "large, round hand"[29] he had learned as a reporter.

He grew so assiduous that he saw everything as news, even the dinner conversation at home. His stepmother hardly dared open her mouth in his presence, for fear of seeing her gossip appear in the *Democrat* the next day; but his father, scornful of Fort's abilities, pressed her to speak, and Fort, with a notebook and pencil in his pocket, scribbled away.[30]

He went to Lake Champlain again, and wrote a story about it, describing a night trip over the lake in the big war canoe. Standish said, "Execrable," a word Fort admired and used in his next piece; but it turned out he meant the handwriting, for the story was published with only a few changes.

He was put on the courthouse beat, and learned to deal with judges, clerks, bailiffs, city officials, political bosses. He experimented with drinking and gambling. He began to write odd, quirky little feature stories, which he found he could sell to a New York syndicate and to the Brooklyn *World.* He was only seventeen.

In the winter of 1891 he paid an unannounced visit to Clarence at Berkshire Farm (referred to in *Many Parts* as "the Industrial Farm"). Clarence was just thirteen; he had been at the farm for three years.

Like Tom Sawyer liberating Nigger Jim, Fort made an elaborate melodrama out of this journey. He got off the train at the stop beyond Canaan and walked back three miles; this seemed more clandestine and exciting than merely getting off at Canaan. The result was that it was dark by the time he got there, and he had to stay all night in a hotel: but that was all right, too.

> You see, we could not tell what we might do when we should see the little kid after having not seen him in such a long time. In our hip pocket there was a revolver. We had always felt contempt for auxiliary weapons, but Biff Allen . . . had pressed this revolver upon us. And the little kid was brought to us. Just as little as ever, but

> sturdy as ever, showing not a sign of ill-treatment except his twitching eye caused in his own home.
>
> All we said was, "How are you?"
>
> All the little kid said was, "Pretty well, I thank you," just as if we were a stranger. But he sort of leaned toward us. And we were seized upon because of that sort of leaning. Our arm around him, having him sit beside us.[31]

The proprietress, here referred to as Mrs. Dean, made polite conversation. Fort asked if Clarence could walk to the station with him, but Mrs. Dean feared not; Clarence had lessons to make up. Outmaneuvered, Fort went away, but came back after dark and climbed a trellis to Clarence's room. Clarence handed him a stolen piece of cake. Moved almost to tears, Fort wrapped it up "to keep forever." They went back to Fort's hotel and talked of escaping to Singapore, but in the end Fort took him back to Berkshire Farm. There is no record that they ever met again.

Clarence was released from Berkshire Farm, probably in 1892. After that his character does not seem to have improved. In a letter dated July 30, 1912, Raymond wrote to Charles, "I have just had the pleasure of meeting Clarence and being called every vile name that mortal man could invent, but I held my temper. He was very drunk. . . ."

Clarence served in the army during and after the Spanish-American War; he was the only one of the three brothers to see military service. He died in 1917, unmarried, age thirty-eight.

Chapter Two

Thirty Thousand Miles (1892–1909)

"Sure, Mrs. Maheffy, ma'am," said Katie, "what do you make work for yourself for? We can eat the vegetables off of the same plates."

"Indeed!"—haughtily—"you find us as we always live; we always have separate dishes for the vegetables. Please don't say plates to me, Miss Dunphy. Call them dishes. I couldn't eat a thing, at the thought of plates to eat off of."

The Outcast Manufacturers

Charles Hoy Fort, eighteen years old, was doing a man's work. He smoked, drank, gambled; he probably consorted with fallen women. (In his account of the visit to Berkshire Farm, he speaks of wishing he could wander through the hills with "our latest Madeline.") He may have considered himself an adult; if so, this view was not shared by his father.

The last quarrel came in 1892; once again, it was over a piece of cake. Fort's wife told the story many years later, in an interview with Theodore Dreiser.

> Charles was a wild kid. He could not bear to be told he must do anything. . . . When Ray wanted to go out, he would go and suck around and cry to his stepmother. But Charlie said to hell with them. Charlie came home one night at ten o'clock, and found he was locked out. The house had a big red glass door, and he took a stone and smashed every bit of the glass. They made him sleep in the basement with the servants, and when he came up, they would not let him have breakfast with the family for a week. The servants were forbidden to pass him anything, but when the cake came around one day, he made a grab for the plate, and the stepmother tried to grab it away from him. Charlie took the cake and threw it at his stepmother. Then there was a fight.

This was the year after Peter V. Fort died, leaving contingent legacies to all three boys; the court appointed a guardian, Matthew J. Wallace, to look after their interests.

Charles was sent to live with his maternal grandfather, John Hoy, but did not stay long.[32] He left school without graduating and went to New York, where he got a job on the Brooklyn *World.* The following year, two ex-*World* men started a suburban weekly in Queens, the Woodhaven *Independent,* and made him editor; but the paper died in infancy. Then Charles Fort, on an allowance of twenty-five dollars a month from his guardian, set out to travel around the world. He tells why in this account, from the Albany *Argus* of April 11, 1909:

> I was born in Albany, N.Y. in 1874, and went to school there as long as they'd let me, and stayed in Albany as long as was practicable. I went to other places, and didn't find much encouragement to stay there.
>
> I've been a tramp and an editor; reporter, joke-writer, fireman, cattleman, book agent, stoker, dishwasher—and what of it? Read the literary notices of other writers, and see how conventional and quite the ordinary thing that is.
>
> I've knocked about the world a little; that's the best I can think of. Started out, when I was nineteen, to wander with a definite purpose. Traveled for two years; made a tangled line on the map, thirty thousand miles long; Nova Scotia and New Orleans; Scotland, Wales and South Africa; all this on an income of twenty-five dollars a month; all this to accumulate an experience and knowledge of life that would fit me to become a writer; wanted to know cowboys and day laborers; sailors, queer boarding house people; clerks, sea captains, vagabonds—everybody. I would get together a vast capital of impressions of life, and then invest it.
>
> An obsession with me; didn't attempt to write anything while preparing; didn't look for a single job or diversion of any kind; nothing but such planning as how to get from Jacksonville to Tampa; how to get from Liverpool to London, and how to live the month out there; treasuring

and hoarding my experiences; a miser in miles; gloating over them—like—"Now, I've got fourteen thousand eight hundred and seventy-five; blue ones, with white foam scattered on them; green miles, through palm trees; yellow, over sandy stretches; black miles, of nights on top of freight cars—now, if I can get from here (Mobile) to New Orleans, that will make it an even fifteen thousand. Up the Mississippi, to Louisville, will be sixteen hundred more."

Southern negroes, with their tatters and turbans; the white cabs of Cape Town, driven by coolies in red fezes; the brown sails of fishing vessels off the high, green-spread coast of Ireland; the pelicans of Tampa; a seal in the Bay of Fundy; the glare of a steamer's wood fire on the banks of the Mississippi; going up the Firth of Clyde, with a white village on one side and a red village on the other; the Peak of Teneriffe, with zones impaled upon it; St. Helena, not only where Napoleon had been, but an African island, where coconuts, dates, olives and bananas grow wild, just like pictures in the geographies. These things that I was seeing! the mania and the sensuous abandon of it! doing not another thing in the world but storing away experiences and impressions. Letters of warning to me, becoming fewer and ceasing. All this, and never mind anything else, to fit myself for writing. Did meet cowboys; did sleep in fo'c's'les; knew carpenters and filibusters and everybody else—had a friend who was a prizefighter; Jameson Raid; saw his belt brought back to Cape Town; bullet hole in it. The excitement of Cape Town, when the raid was on; factory whistles blowing at midnight.

Experiences that you might find material in? Going up the Mississippi; six dollars from New Orleans to Louisville; find own food and no good fishing; sleep wherever I wanted to, if I wanted to where I was wanted to. Sleeping one night on a pile of cypress lumber; don't know why, because cotton bales and molasses barrels were plentiful; awakened away in the night by nibbling feeling at my ankles; a roustabout trying to steal the shoes from my feet; probably remonstrated with him. No hardships; picturesqueness transmuting everything; maybe within a few months I could begin to use the material I was collecting.

Had fifteen cents and two friends in Mobile, twenty-five dollars waiting for me in the New Orleans post office. Two friends left behind by their boss, who always traveled like a passenger. He enlarged photographs, and they canvassed for him. Between us and New Orleans, about one hundred and forty miles of swamps. Think highly of friendship, have read, with approbation, poetry about it, but got crackers and cheese with the fifteen cents. Three of us on the way to New Orleans. Fourteen miles out, and a watering tank; freight cars stopping. Brakeman coming along the board walk on a car top and looking at us; didn't know if he cared for cheese, and had some diffidence in offering him a cracker. "Oh, that's all right!" said the brakeman. "Then we can get to New Orleans, can we?" "Sure! you'll get to New Orleans; don't let that worry you." Most amiable brakeman; an addition to the fund of characters; would write about him some day. One of us nervous, and repeating: "Then we're bound right through, are we?" "You're as good as there; don't worry."

Black night, and the yellow swath of the headlight; glimpses of the gulf surf in long, white lines; the fluttering of hanging moss on the trees around us. "The only thing," said the brakeman, "is that you'll have to do your ten days, sweeping the streets, in the chain gang. The cops get ten dollars a head for every hobo from a freight car, but you'll get to New Orleans; don't let that part worry you." Scenery and impressions, but spoiled some; had seen a chain gang in Richmond, and it did seem so conspicuous. Almost to New Orleans; fast freight and bad jumping; three of us to be linked like zebra sausages—shriek from another engine, and our train stopping at a crossing—oh, let the chain gang go; one should not be too avaricious for experiences.

From Louisville, apparently, Fort continued northward and took ship from Nova Scotia, probably to Glasgow. From there he went by rail to London, then traveled in western England and Wales. Returning to London, he took ship for Capetown, calling at Teneriffe (in the Canaries) and St. Helena on the way.

Tramping through Lancashire one Sunday morning; had three ha'pence; price of one mild ale; stopping at a public house; had never heard of the Sunday law, by which one who has come a distance greater than three miles may get a drink. "Where'd you come from?" the publican. "From New York." "Bli' me! you've come far enough!" drawing one.

Went to sleep one night in England, under a culvert; rush and roar of the passing trains; tracks three feet away. Didn't have any money, but such plans of a thousand here and five thousand there when the time should come for the investing of all this accumulating capital. Rush and roar that, under the bridge, became frenzy; peacefulness and comfort; had found, in the dark, some kind of soft material to lie on. Scream of an engine, and time to get up in the morning. Never liked to get up in the morning; this time, couldn't; one shoulder up a little, but other seeming to drag; well, will power; that's the only way to get up in the morning; will power all very well, but something holding fast to an elbow. Oh, dear me, never since caught a fly on fly paper; sympathy. Had gone to sleep on the contents of a broken tar barrel. Tar and warm-blooded animal; result of contiguity. It's a cruel thing to catch flies on fly paper. Never mind, more seen of the world every day; rewards coming soon now.

Traveling from Glasgow to London; stopping at a station with something to eat in it; price of a sandwich. Got out and worried over ham or chicken—train gliding away; all the doors locked—oh, my! my! compartment with own luggage long gone by, and train going faster—sudden energy; great presence of mind in emergency—head first through a window and the protecting chest of the austere and pompous kind of an elderly Englishman. Broke his eyeglasses, knocked his book out the window, spilled the bottle of cold tea he was drinking. Had done enough damage to raise anybody's indignation. The Englishman's resentment: "Sir, this is a most undignified entrance!" And luggage on ahead, and who could tell in which compartment? Never mind; had the sandwich. London; luggage never recovered. Never mind; bought another collar.

Had a good home once; looked very promising; had just the kind of a garret that had often longed for; and two rats who had not a trace of snobbishness in them. A "gentleman-farmer" had taken self in from the road; interested in self, and was going to make something of him; don't know which, gentleman or farmer. Was a squire, too; very interesting; had never seen a squire before; more capital. First morning, Squire got on his horse to ride to his office, in Liverpool; gave self a pair of spurs to polish; mentioned a garden, with weeds in it, perhaps, or said something about a hoe somewhere. Self didn't know so very much about work in those days. Squire back in the evening; self still polishing the spurs. Yet one hears of the rewards of perseverance; lost good home on account of it, a romantic garret, and two rats who weren't inclined to draw social distinctions. Not much of a story, that! But read some of those about others who have books published.

Then came the end of two years. I had thirty thousand, many-colored, vividly diversified miles hoarded; experiences, impressions, hundreds of characters, the world's scenery. Nothing more to see; everything in life known; only twenty-one years old, but now for the work of a master! Here, in New York, I met an old man, whose side was paralyzed, so that he never left his rooms, where he lived with wife and daughter. I boasted to him of all that I had seen, and all that I had learned. He said: "I too, have always had that interest in life. When I got on the cars, I thought that at last I had got where I could study and understand human nature; such opportunities; the thousands of people, on and off, every minute; all ages, occupations and temperaments; here was wealth of material for me. Lord! Lord! such a mistake. You don't want to know something about everybody, but everything about somebody. I never began to learn about life until I was cooped up here with my wife and Maggie."

Then I, with my thirty thousand miles, and the hundreds of characters; the impressions of houses, roads, waves, coasts, and people! One cannot ignore a truth when one has passed through all the errors below it. The toppling of the structure that two of my best years had gone into. Pelicans of Tampa, Poets' Corner, in Westminster Abbey, the bow of a vessel cutting waves, at night time. All gone, and no investing of capital; I knew that one should not scatter one's self upon all life, but centre upon some one kind of life and know it thoroughly. Romances that would have to be sordidified into

> the doings of some little group of commonplace people. Nothing more of headlights of engines in Southern forests, but the lighting of the fire in Mrs. Murphy's back kitchen; Mamie Murphy, and her young man, and a few neighbors.
>
> Thus ended my first lesson. It takes me about two years to learn anything. As, in writing, there are so many things to be learned, besides concentration, one might overlook the crudities in the book that I am about to have published.[33] I have spent only thirteen years of continuous effort, after first learning something.
>
> Snapshots? Ever since, I have lived nowhere but in rear houses and back tenements, so I never have known anybody with a camera. No one has ever taken a snapshot of me; if he had it would be unconventional enough to suit you.

In South Africa, it appears, Fort had contracted "a fever"—malaria, maybe.[34] Ill and alone in New York, he met Anna Filing, an English girl he had known in Albany. She nursed him back to health, and Fort married her on October 26, 1896, when he was twenty-two and she was twenty-six.

Anna, born in Sheffield, had been sent to live with relatives in Albany when she was a girl. She had known Fort since he was thirteen. "I always loved him," she told Dreiser later, "but never thought I would marry him."

For their wedding trip they went to Maine, where there was "not a drop of drink."

> Charlie was not much of a drinking fellow, but he went out to buy tickets for Canada, and

> was gone the longest time. He had thirty dollars with him. After hours and hours I heard his voice, and I looked out the window and there he was. You never saw such a drunken boy. He was arm in arm with a man in overalls, and the man was saying, "I'm a gentleman, even if I am in overalls." He wanted Charlie to lend him some money, but he was cagey enough. He said, "I'll have to ask my wife." I came down, and I was so mad, and disgusted with him that I took him by the shoulders and spanked him all the way upstairs.[35]

Fort was six feet tall, burly and strong. Anna was a birdlike little woman, not more than five feet four.

In New York, Fort and Anna took the cheapest lodgings they could find. Later he was to have a small income from securities and real estate, but for years the young couple lived on the edge of poverty. His relatives visited them seldom, believing Fort had "married beneath him."[36] Anna was not a literary person; "She never read his, or any other books," said Tiffany Thayer;[37] but we know that her cooking was good, and Fort, in his letters, frequently praises her home brew.

From his grandfather Fort had inherited a house in Albany, but it brought them little income, and from 1898 on they were making desperate attempts to sell it.

In 1901 Anna was seriously ill. We have two touching letters Fort wrote to her,[38] and a receipt from German Hospital on Seventy-seventh Street for fourteen dollars.

In the following year, Fort was dismissed by the manager of the Metropolitan Hotel. His recommendation, dated June 2, says that Fort had been employed there for eight months, had "made himself useful in the kitchen," and was "honest and sober." On the same day Fort applied for a job as watchman at the Hotel Buckingham. The referral slip, from the Grand Central Employment Agency, is marked, "Not engaged." In October of that year Fort pawned something for thirty-one cents. The scrawl on the pawnbroker's receipt looks like "2 Suits."

Poverty in New York in the 1900s was no joke. There were times when Fort and Anna had no firewood but broken chairs; Fort could not go out to hunt for work when it rained, because of the holes in his shoes.[39]

Some of the tenements they lived in must have been in Irish neighborhoods, like the house Fort describes in a story called "A Great Human Principle":[40]

> A three-story house. An old yellow house. Clapboards patched here and there and the patches painted when put up, so that the front of the house was tessellated with squares, some vivid, some dull, some of almost obliterated yellow paint. Brick sidewalk and a paling fence between it and the house. Worn-out grass behind the fence, and creeping out in tufts between bricks. Weather-worn shutters, some open, and some tied shut with dangling pieces of clothes-line. Tenement region of New York.
>
> On the top floor lived the Boyles; second floor, Mrs. Cassidy; first floor, Mrs. Ryan—no polyglot house here, you see; not a Schwartzenheimer nor a Tortolini in it, but straight Boyle, Cassidy and Ryan from top to bottom.

These tenements were not like the sterile middle-class apartment buildings of modern New York, where you may live and die without knowing who your neighbors are. They were like villages, with women running up and down the stairs to tell the latest scandals about each other.

> And sinks in houses like this . . . are very much like wells in Oriental countries—meeting places, gossiping places for women.
>
> Mrs. Lunn at the third-floor sink; Mrs. Delaney at the next sink; Mrs. Weasel at the first-floor sink.
>
> And pretty Mrs. Delaney, the motorman's wife!—starting to run up to the sink above, but feeling that something more interesting might be said at the sink below. Starting, then, to run down to the first sink, but feeling that Mrs. Lunn would be less guarded in her utterances, as she was not likely to stay in the house very much longer. Face like a mouse's, most of it nose! But a mouse has a nice, bright, little face, you know. Mouse-like nose sniffing for news up the stairs and sniffing for news down the stairs.
>
> All three women suffering intensely! One must gossip, but one must have some excuse, if only the borrowing of a match, to approach the relief of gossiping. All three women crying:
>
> "Oh, Mrs. Delaney, excuse me if I'm taking the water away from you! Mrs. Lunn, I only want a drop for the kettle. Never mind, Mrs. Weasel, the pressure is so bad today, I'll have to come down to your sink, anyway." They get together. Trust them for that when it was necessary to their happiness to discuss Mrs. Bonti-

cue! All three of them up and at it! "Outrageous! Oh, scandalous! Never heard of such carryings-on before!" Turning on the water, at least pretending to fill a kettle. "We ought of complained on her long ago! She'll feel flat enough when she gets her dispossess! But the assurance of her! Well, she'll have a different look when she gets her notice to go!" A pause long enough to empty a kettle so as to fill it again. And then:

"But suppose she wins him over! What if he don't put her out! She'll own us! The top floor will own us! and there'll be no living in the house. Suppose!"

Eviction was a normal hazard of tenement life; it turns up repeatedly in Fort's stories and in his novel, *The Outcast Manufacturers.* In "Ructions," from which the quotation above is taken, a wonderful old fraud, Mrs. Bonticue, having received her dispossess notice, calls in friends and neighbors for a housebreaking party. They begin with bricks.

. . . ladies and gentlemen bearing fragments of the tottering old chimney came tumbling down from the roof.

"What mind if we was disorderly people!" Clatter and bang all the way down the stairs!

"Us always so decorous and the pink of propriety we was!" Ashes heaped high in every sink. Ashes strewn up and down the stairs.

Back to the room and from Mrs. Bonticue:

"Whisper, once I lost a dime down the crack of this floor. And you'd think I'd leave a dime

> behind for any landlord to enjoy? I'll have what belongs to me, as is no more than right."
>
> And, with a crowbar of Willie's, Aleck Bonticue had to rip up the floor, to make everything agreeable at home. Up with the flooring and beams pitched down into the back yard.
>
> Yes, we hear a good deal of the sadness of dispossession cases—they are sad.[41]

Fort continued to sell feature stories to New York newspapers for a time, then branched out into fiction. In 1905, Theodore Dreiser recalled, "Fort came to me [at *Smith's Magazine*] with the best humorous short stories that I have ever seen produced in America. I purchased some of them. Some of his writings suggested mental clowning, but they were realistic, ironic, wise and in their way, beautiful. I think I published six or seven. And other editors did the same. And among ourselves—Richard Duffy of Tom Watson's, Charles Agnew MacLean of *The Popular Magazine*, and others, we loved to talk of him and his future—a new and rare literary star."[42]

At about the same time he began writing novels. Year in and year out, he said, he wrote novels—"3,500,000 words, though that's only an estimate."[43] If these novels averaged seventy thousand words, he must have written fifty. Say that he wrote five drafts of each; then, at any rate, there must have been ten novels. Only one was ever published.

In a financial sense, then, but in no other, Fort was an unsuccessful writer of fiction. He wrote with warmth and humor of the New York he knew, a place that is now almost as alien to us as Mars. He wrote of a time of poverty and exuberance, a time when there was still such a thing as "the Irish."

Mauve decade, my eye. Here is the grimy, vigorous, shouting reality:

> Paddy's Market! Every Saturday, though not fully epileptic with writhing and squirming, groan and convulsion, until evening, Ninth Avenue, from Forty-second Street to Thirty-eighth Street, is a market place. Wagons and stands, each wagon and each stand with a torch, or with several torches, so that, from a distance, Paddy's Market looks like a torchlight parade going up one side of the avenue and down the other side—a night parade of flagellants shrieking with self-inflicted torture.
>
> Then, heard in the market itself, confused lamentation disintegrates into distinct and mercantile cries—flagellants scourging themselves only with their arms, beating their breasts only to keep warm—to rid themselves not of sin, but of cauliflowers and beets.
>
> Crowd on the sidewalk marching down the avenue, eight abreast—ranks of fours tripping down, and fours struggling up—bold front of nine sweeping up—single files penetrating down; individuals filtering down—up current again dominating, surging and thrusting back.[44]

Or here, in "Ructions":

> A New York street! Looking like a progressive battle-field.
>
> On a windy day, trust to the ash-man to

make any street look like a battle-field or the route of a Russian grand duke's afternoon drive. Up on his knee with a barrel; up on the wheel with it; into the cart with the ashes, any way at all, and up and out with a cloud of dust as if from a bomb explosion. Smaller explosions suggested along both sides of the street; women seeing the cart coming and running out of tenements to empty pans in barrels, knocking pans against barrels to shake loose clinging particles; puffs of dust gushing forth; unfortunate passers-by rubbing their eyes frantically.

Children everywhere! Making swings of clothes-lines tied to cross-arms of lamp-posts; winding their ropes around posts, revolving in sinking spirals, with ropes unwinding. And skipping ropes, trying to count up to a hundred without feet catching; ropes swiftly beating the sidewalk so that skippers should fail to count up to one hundred.

An old horse, looking as if about ready to be set for dinner; large table cloth, in place of a blanket, on him. Old horse standing in front of a cellar with a sign, "I Don't Buy From No Children."[45]

Fort's eye for the incongruous and unexpected, his perception of hidden relationships, was already evident. In a story called "Twenty Campers," he wrote:

Watermelons were undulating in a green streak from a cart to the rear of Leonidas Marcy's store. Men in a line caught melons with a sharp slap on each side, and turned just in time

> to catch another, . . . catching and throwing in one motion.[46]

Anyone could have seen the men and the melons. Fort saw the green streak—the pattern of motion made visible.

He was still struggling against poverty. In February, 1906, his guardian Matthew J. Wallace got him a five-hundred-dollar mortgage on the Albany house, but the money did not last long. In December of that year, Wallace wrote to him: ". . . Your tenants do not pay until about the middle of the month, and since, I sent you the last money I have paid out some $15.— for topping out chimney & carpenter work in connection with plumber. So therefore we are 'busted' up here also. However to help you out, in your distress, and save a distinguished and useful life I enclose check for $20.—."

In the same year, in November, Wallace had written this significant letter: ". . . I know considerable of your private life, and the family. It is sad—but more so, to know the intense feeling you harbor. You have cause, and it is human to be bitter, I confess, but Charley, dont cultivate that hatred, endeavor to live it down (if it will down)."

In December, 1907, Fort wrote in his diary: "Have not been paid for one story since May. Have two dollars left. Watson's has cheated me out of $155. Dreiser has sent back two stories he told me he would buy, one even advertised to appear in his next number. There will be no money from the house next month. I owe $15 since July on the mortgage. Everything is pawned. W. [Wallace?] led me to believe he would buy the house and now backs out. I am unable to write. I can do nothing else for a living. My mind is filled with pictures of myself cutting my throat or leaping out the window, head first."

The old bitterness between Fort and his father had not changed. In March, 1912, when Charles Nelson Fort was abed with the ailment that was killing him, he wrote to his son:

> Dear Sir—
>
> Observe the style of address. . . . I had been more cordial had you not set the pace for me but your CNFort was too cold. I will endeavor to answer your letter seriatim *et brevitum*—How does that hit you? Paragraph number one rehearses my recovery. I regret to write that I am not better but worse. I fear that my case is incurable. . . .

He had cerebral meningitis. Blanche Fort, Charles's stepmother, had gone blind.

Charles Nelson Fort died June 27, 1912, aged sixty-three. In his will, he left his whole estate to Blanche for the term of her life; on her death, the estate was to go to Raymond, or, if Raymond was dead, to any children he might have. In the event that Raymond died without surviving children, then Charles, the eldest son, was to share equally with Clarence, the youngest. Blanche died in 1913 and Raymond inherited.

Fort kept on writing. Now he had dropped short stories in favor of novels, thinking that "except in the writing of novels, which probably looked like the offspring of kangaroos, not an incentive could there be to go on living."[47]

His one published novel is *The Outcast Manufacturers* (New York, B. W. Dodge Co., 1909). The ugly title probably contributed to its neglect, but it makes perfect sense when you have read the book. The "Manufacturers" are Mr. Birtwhistle, his wife and entourage, who operate "a minute semi-fraudulent mail-order business"[48] until they are evicted and find themselves on the street. Birtwhistle's enterprise is called the Universal Manufacturing Company, but in fact all he does is to send out catalogs listing the products of other mail-order companies, and forward any orders he gets. The merchandise, which Birtwhistle and his employees never see, sometimes arouses their curiosity:

> "And," said Miss Guffy, "the Great Ten-cent Packages! I'd like to see what's in that, myself. We've sold dozens; I wonder what's in that. The Fighting Roosters and the Frightful Rattlesnakes and the Jumbo Microbe Finder—I'll not rest in my grave if I don't find out what that Great Ten-cent Package contains. Sure, what could it be?"[49]

If Birtwhistle is like anybody else in literature, it is Dickens's Micawber, or perhaps the White Knight in *Alice*—gentle, impractical, kindly, full of wild enthusiasms alternating with deepest despairs. "I must have my own enterprise. Am I a mere machine to work for some one else?—though for a young man to do so is the only way to acquire experience. I was never born to be the serf of an alarm-clock, but, when I get up in the morning, to take a spin in my auto or a canter on horseback, before breakfast, whenever weather permits."[50]

"The book," Anthony Boucher wrote, "deserves attention which it has never received as a purely realistic genre novel well ahead of its time—objective, unromanticized, and observed with acute eyes and ears closer to those of Ring Lardner or Sinclair Lewis than the average novelist of 1909."[51] All this is true, but *The Outcast Manufacturers* is much more: it is a comic fantasy, a kind of novelistic Punch and Judy show. By a trick of perspective, Fort has put his characters into a shoebox stage and made them seem like tiny engaging puppets, dressed in scraps, with faces the size of buttons.

In chapter one, when Sim, the young man from the country, enters seeking employment, shy Mrs. Birtwhistle runs "to an inner room, through a doorway, where blue curtains, meeting at top, dwindled away from each other, like overalls of a straddling giant."[52] Even the distinction between the characters and the furniture is sometimes blurred: The second Miss Dunphy, one of Mrs. Birtwhistle's two nieces, is "a straight-up-and-down young person, dressed in white. Had she stood very still, with her big colorless, round face, she might possibly have been mistaken for an aquarium globe on a marble pedestal."[53] And: "She flushed a little—flushes, like goldfish in an aquarium, fluttering in her globe-like, colorless face—goldfish in a globe of milk, perhaps—or goldfish struggling in a globe of whitewash, have it."[54]

Sometimes the distortion of perspective goes in the other direction, as in this about Mrs. Birtwhistle: "Her two little teeth, like side-by-side aprons of waitresses, far away."[55] Or this, about an upstairs neighbor: "—heavy dark nostrils of Mrs. Tunnan; nose like a tiny model of a subway entrance; nostrils almost perpendicular and shaped like soles of tiny feet; soles of the feet of a fairy, rest of him investigating within."[56]

When the mail orders run out and the eviction notice comes, Birtwhistle, Sim, and the silent, bearlike Mr. Parker sleep on park benches, wrapping themselves in newspaper as Mr. Parker shows them. Miss Guffy, the sharp-tongued little hunchback, has gone God knows where; Mrs. Birtwhistle has taken a job in a hotel, working twelve hours a day.

One clue strongly suggests that Mrs. Birtwhistle, in this episode, is Anna Fort. Among Fort's papers I found an undated letter, handwritten in a hasty scrawl:

> My dear Annie,
>
> We are busted. I must see you to talk about selling the house. Be on the corner of Eighth Avenue and Forty sixth street at half past eight, tonight.
>
> Very truly yours,
> Charles Fort

If this were all, the letter might have no particular importance. But the words "at half past eight" have been crossed out, and in their place is written, "Right now."

The letter could not have been mailed; it must have been handed to someone, to be passed on to Anna, in a place Fort could not enter. If I am right about this, the following passage is from the life.

> "Easy, is it? Down forty feet below the sidewalk, standing all day on a little box, shaking linen, and, if you step down, burn your feet on the steam pipes, when your shoes is bad. Not but what some of the old hands has it easy. Like Margaret, who tries on the bellboys' gloves; just sits and shapes them on her hands so they make quick changes. It isn't the work, but the rotten people you meet. At dinner, all of them

> grabbing at a loaf of bread, tearing out inside chunks and leaving the crust; and the girl on the waiting! You ask her to pass something, and she hollers: 'Will you have it now or wait till you get it?' and you going to another table, where the girl says: 'You dare take anything from here, and I'll smash you in the puss!' and nothing for dinner but the heads and tails of herrings, the middles gone to the officers' tables; or the necks and gizzards of chickens, boiled to rags, for soup. . . . Or when you try to sleep, to be up at six in the morning, and the late watch comes in, laughing and carrying on, and won't let you sleep, because they don't have to report till eleven next day. Or some beast you sleep with! She comes in late, soused; she comes into bed with you, in silk waist, hat and shoes—'Get up, woman, and have some decency about you!'—she snores. 'Woman, get up; your hat-pins is sticking me!' She says: 'I'll have to sleep with all me clothes on; I must be up for mass at six in the morning.'"[57]

Fort has so often been described as a hermit that people forget he was a newspaper reporter. He lived most of his life in tenements, and he had a sociable wife. He knew his New York—the tenements, the docks, warehouses, saloons. He did not see its inhabitants quite as anyone else saw them, but he knew and loved them; he had learned the lesson of "Mamie Murphy, and her young man, and a few neighbors."

His novel is full of gentle surprises. The silent Mr. Asbury Parker, who all through the Manufacturers' homeless wanderings has kept with him a bundle of his wife's letters, explains in chapter fourteen.

> . . . "These are all I got in the world, Birt."
> "It isn't everybody who'd carry around old letters so."
> "But these are from my wife, Birt."
> "Sometimes I feel sorry for you, Asbury."
> "They're not all letters; most of them are postal cards. Yes, Birt—"
> "Go ahead, Asbury."
> "Yes, Birt, if she ever sues me for non-support, I'll come back at her for sending me these defamatory postal cards."
> "Don't I tell you!" cried the admiring Captain. "Mr. Parker don't speak often, but when he does, he's worth listening to!"[58]

In chapter twelve Mrs. Birtwhistle has slipped out of the hotel at night to see her husband. With Sim and Parker, they are walking up Fifth Avenue. Mrs. Birtwhistle stops to look at an uncurtained second-story window.

> A man was sitting by a table with a lamp on it. A woman was fiercely shaking her fist at him. "She's giving it to him—wait!" laughed Mrs. Birtwhistle. The woman slapping a palm with a fist—the man feebly waving a hand at her. Woman turning her back to him, turning and running back, screeching at him; man with his head on his arms.
> "We don't want to stand here all night, do we?" asked Mr. Birtwhistle.

"Just wait! Let's watch them!" said fascinated Mrs. Birtwhistle.

Man looking up, and his hands moving in weak, apologetic gestures. Woman stamping and pounding her fist upon the table, then pointing at him and shaking a fierce forefinger at him, throwing arms wide to express scorn and contempt for him, and then again shaking her fist at him.

"Oh, I'm homesick! I'm as homesick as I can be!" wept Mrs. Birtwhistle.[59]

Chapter Three

X and *Y* (1910–1918)

> Of what is significant in one's own existence one is hardly aware. . . . What does a fish know about the water in which he swims all his life?
>
> Albert Einstein, *Out of My Later Years*

In early photographs we see him as a sturdy young man, somewhat plump-faced, with curly hair and an absurd pince-nez, a little like Teddy Roosevelt. In later pictures he has a heavy mustache; his features have smoothed out somehow, become wider, more regular; his eyes are calm. Fort was tall, strongly built like his brother Raymond, who was a bear of a man. He may have got his size and strength from some remote Vandervoort, but his father was slim and elegant; his paternal grandfather, P. V. Fort, looked like a lean Yankee trader. I'm inclined to think that his big frame, his snub nose, his calm, bold eyes came from old John Hoy, his mother's father.

Tiffany Thayer gives this somewhat imaginative picture of him, in the introduction to *The Books of Charles Fort:*

> He was nearly if not quite six feet tall, heavy, fair. He wore a brown mustache that bristled somewhat less than Nietzsche's. His sight was failing in his last years and his glasses had to be thick-lensed. He was an anachronism in modern dress, incongruous in his Bronx flat. As we sat with home brew of his making, strong cheeses, coarse rye bread and "whiskied grapes" at a circular dining table, talking the night away, it often occurred to me that his frame called for leather and buckles, that the board should have been bare and brown, washed by slops from heavy tankards and worn smooth by heavy sword-hands. The light should have been from flambeaux and—to match our words—Faust and Villon should have stopped by in passing on their way to murder or conference with the devil.[60]

This magniloquence would have made Fort smile, I think. He was no Viking or medieval knight, and had no yearning for piratical adventure. He was the mildest and kindest of men. He had had some disappointments, but had learned to laugh at them. He had withdrawn from the world, not because he hated human beings, but, I think, because he did not want to injure them.

Something of his kindliness, and of his solitary life,

comes through in this passage of *New Lands* which he wrote in his last year:

> A neighbor had pigeons, and the pigeons landed on my window sill. They were tempted to come in, but for weeks, stretched necks, fearing to enter. I wished they would come in. I went four blocks to get them sunflower seeds. Though I will go thousands of miles for data, it is most unusual for me to go four blocks—it's eight blocks, counting both ways—for anybody. One time I found three of them, who had flown through an open window, and were upon the frame of a closed window. I went to them slowly, so as not to alarm them. It seems that I am of a romantic disposition, and, if I take a liking to anybody, who seems female, like almost all birds, I want her to perch on my finger. So I put out a finger. But all three birds tried to fly through the glass. They could not learn, by rebuffs, but kept on trying to escape through the glass. If, back in the coop, these pigeons could have told their story, it would have been that they were perched somewhere, when suddenly the air hardened. Everything in front was as clearly visible as before, but the air had suddenly turned impenetrable. Most likely the other pigeons would have said: "Oh, go tell that to the sparrows!"
>
> There is a moral in this, and it applies to a great deal in this book, which is upon the realization of wishes. I had wished for pigeons. I got them. After the investigation by the three pioneers all of them came in. There were nine

> of them. It was the unusually warm summer of 1931, and the windows had to be kept open. Pigeons on the backs of chairs. They came up on the table, and inspected what I had for dinner. Other times they spent on the rug, in stately groups and processions, except every now and then, when they were not so dignified. I could not shoo them out, because I had invited them. Finally, I did get screens: but it takes weeks to be so intelligent. So the moral is in the observation that, if you wish for something, you had better look out, because you may be so unfortunate as to get it. . . . Much is said of the "cruelty of Nature": but, when a man is denied his "heart's desire," that is mercy.[61]

There must have been neighbors in and out of the apartment all day long; and I like to imagine that Fort smiled at them, as he smiled at the pigeons strutting up and down the carpet; gave them his attention, while they were there, and, when they were gone, went back to his own thoughts.

"One time when I was down worst I ever have been," he wrote to Dreiser, "I was studying the infinitesimal calculus. Every morning, I'd try to write something that would bring in some money; every morning, by ten o'clock, I was back studying transcendental functions and things. It's utterly past my power to do things I feel I ought to do."[62]

He did what he was driven to do. He read enormously; he took notes and filled a wall of pigeonholes with them. He read himself out of his dubious belief in scientific infallibility, and into a half-belief in scientific chimeras. He destroyed his notes. "Nevertheless, the power, or the hypnosis, of them, orthodox notes, all of them, orthodox materialism, Tyndall says this, Darwin says that, authoritativeness, positiveness, chemists and astronomers and geologists have proved this or that, nevertheless, monism and revolt were making me write that not even are twice two four, except arbitrarily and conventionally. . . ."[63]

Because he believed there were, in science, only believers and cranks, and because he would not be a believer, he became a crank. He read Americus Symmes's book about the hollow Earth,[64] and Charles Piazzi Smyth's book about the pyramids,[65] and in the New York Public Library he looked at Otto Hahn's *Die Meteorite, Chondrite, und Ihre Organismen,* with its sepia-colored plates of microscopic inclusions, looking like tiny corals, in meteorites. He wrote a crank book of his own, and called it *X.* Then he wrote another, called *Y.* Neither was ever published, and the manuscripts, like nearly all Fort's manuscripts, were destroyed; but we still have the letters he wrote Dreiser about them.

X was organized around the notion that our civilization is invisibly controlled by beings on the planet Mars (anticipating Fort's famous line, "I think we're property"). In *Y,* Fort imagined another sinister civilization, a little closer at hand—at the South Pole. He considered that Kaspar Hauser, the mysterious boy who appeared in Nuremberg in 1828, was an emissary from "Y-land," and that he was murdered to prevent his revealing the truth.

I would give a great deal if someone would magically produce the manuscripts of these two books, along with Fort's lost novels and God knows what else that went into the fire, or the trash heap, some time or other. All the same, and in spite of Dreiser's enthusiasm for *X* and *Y*, it does not surprise me that no one would publish them.

The excesses of these two books are excesses of belief, or of quasi-belief. Fort was still hampered by the orthodoxy of the unorthodox; in rejecting conventional systems, he felt obliged to set up his own unconventional ones and defend them. He did this, I think, because he knew of no other way to write an unorthodox book. This was the way others had done it, the only way it had been done; and he had yet to invent his own way.

In 1915 Dreiser, who was dickering for a movie job that never materialized, asked Fort to submit ideas for screenplays, and Fort said he would try. He added, however, "Swear to me that I needn't write love stories. If lovers there must be, let someone else put the damn things in."[66]

In March, 1916, he wrote to Dreiser enclosing the rough draft of *Y*, and condoling with him for his failure to sell *X*. "Brace up. This is only the beginning. The gods have appointed me, in this life, which is hell, to punish you for something awful that you did once, perhaps in Jupiter or Neptune—'Z' hasn't yet even been heard from. You have at least one thing to be thankful for—I might have begun with 'A.' "[67]

In June he wrote that he had collected so much more data that he wanted to rewrite *Y* completely. He was hampered, he said, by a great calamity that had come upon him.

> My uncle died last Sunday. But that's not the worst. The worst is that my wife, from the best and most helpful woman in the world, has become a snob. She insists that now I must almost always have a clean shirt on. My dear

Dreiser, pity me; I must have my shoes blacked —but I must leave rear houses.

My dear Dreiser, for twenty years, I have lived with strange orthogenetic gods, who are not snobs; who brood over stables and dumps and rear houses. If I desert them, "Z" will never be written, because it was from the great god Syntheticus, himself, that I derived "X" and "Y." But now Amorpha, who, being feminine, scorns dumps and rear houses, has in the past overlooked me, will, in three or four rooms and a bath, have me at her mercy. This matter of a bath room is breaking my heart; my wife insists, but she's playing right into Amorpha's hands. . . .

No, I'm doomed. I must now take my place among barbers and policemen and firemen and their wives, or in fact become a member of a class that in the past has been far, far above me. The Executors of my grandfather's will don't like me, however that has come about, and won't advance me a cent; so I shall have a few months of communion with strange orthogenetic gods; and that time I shall give to "Y."

Then I shall lose my literary soul. There is another part of the estate that comes to me upon the death of an aunt of mine; here there has been such gross mismanagement that I shall have to bring suit. I shall speak to lawyers; strange orthogenetic gods will never forgive me for that.

Pray for me. Have masses said for the repose of my aspirations. It may be that, by means of surreptitious old shirts, that I can hide from

> my wife and rub around on the floor when she's not looking, I may propitiate Syntheticus and the still greater god Equalization; or may be I'll go into that bath room and only splash around the water, and make a noise, but not really get into it–[68]

Fort's uncle, Frank A. Fort, died on May 28, 1916, and part of his share in the estate of Peter V. Fort passed to Charles, Raymond, and Clarence. From this time on, it appears that Fort was financially independent. (When Clarence died in the following year, his share was divided between Charles and Raymond.) In June, 1916, on the strength of this inheritance, Fort borrowed five hundred dollars from a bank in Albany, and in July he and Anna bought some furniture–two rugs, a sofa and two chairs, a set of dishes–total, $180.

In July, threatened with prosecution by the New York Society For the Suppression of Vice (what a charmingly old-fashioned sound that has now!), the publisher of Dreiser's *The "Genius"* had withdrawn all copies from the bookstores. On August 13, Fort wrote:

> High-priest of Evil:
>
> Damn it all! speak to me! tell me! what shall I do to be lewd? . . .
>
> I write of the attractions of the planets, and of the affinities of atoms. These are lusts. Yet, to save me, I can not convey evil notions of astronomic and chemic obscenities. . . .

In a postscript he added:

> Damnation! that damned "Y" is only half re-written.

Dreiser's efforts to find a publisher for Fort continued. He admired *X* tremendously, but perhaps did not quite understand it; at any rate, his description of the book is hard to reconcile with Fort's.

> Fort, in his book, saw certain rays, only he did not call them X or Cosmic, for X was the mysterious something from which these rays were emanating. But what these rays did, and wherein it was that their wonder and power lay, I will try to show. These rays were the emanation of something that was capable *through them as a medium* of creating *us*, you, me, all animals, plants, the earth and its fullness, its beauty and variety and strangeness, its joy and sorrow and terror as well as the ecstasy of this thing we call life in all its variety and scope. And it did this quite as we, by the means of light and photography, throw a moving picture on a screen, the sensitive chemicals of a photographic film and the light that causes that film first to receive an impression of something and later to retransmit it as seemingly the very substance of reality. Only to X, the earth is the sensitive film and its speeding rays the light of the modern film camera.
>
> Of course, all this was interwoven with comments on the history of man, or the dubiousness of his recorded knowledge, the unreliability of his so-called facts, together with much data sufficiently substantiated to seem to be well worth accepting or, if not that, of investigating. Yet all of this, as I personally rise to testify, was in its day consistently and ir-

ritatingly and even insultingly ignored by those to whom I presented it. Yet so impressed was I by all this that shortly after I read his book I had a dream which seemed in no indefinite way to confirm it. And arising from that dream, some months or weeks after I had read the book, I immediately sat down and wrote out a one-act interpretation of it, using Fort's theory as the thesis or backbone of the action. You will find it on pages 60 to 75 in my book *Hey-Rub-a-Dub-Dub.* I entitled that one-act play *The Dream,* and later showed it to Fort. It was nothing like his book in action and less so in effectiveness. For his book had the immense and rugged massiveness of a whole natural and physical scene—the world and all its history, no less—and amazingly substantiated by heaven knows what astounding data, whereas my one-act play was no more than an eight- or nine-page conversation between a few characters in real life and in my dream. Yet even so, my dream was a fairly fortunate adumbration of the central idea of his great work.

"X" was an amazing book and at the time, I thought to myself, "Well here at last is something new—a new mind and a new approach. I can sponsor it." So I went to Macmillan, Harper's, Scribner's, John Lane, but not one of them wanted it. "It's not this and it's not that," they said. And so they rejected it. I asked Fort to leave a copy of the book with me and in due time I would interest a publisher. But no, he wouldn't do that. He took it away, and the next thing he told me was that he had destroyed it and was writing *The Book of the Damned,* and that he would rather I would interest myself in that, which I did, only still believing that "X" was even more wonderful. However, this time I didn't waste time with scientific publications or their editors or just any publisher. Rather I took it—*The Book of the Damned*—direct to my personal publisher, Horace Liveright, and, laying the book on the table, told him to publish it. And when, after a week or so, he announced: "But I can't do it. We'll lose money," I said, "If you don't publish it, you'll lose me." So the book was published.[69]

Fort wrote to thank Dreiser in this elliptical way:

My dear Dreiser:—

I'm very much astonished to learn that you've been talking about me behind my back.

I have just received a note from Boni & Liveright telling me that you've been saying things about me.

But, like most atheists, I'm a good Christian. I not only forgive you, but I have honored you.

I have invented something. I have named it after you.

It's a meatless cocktail.

You take a glass of beer, and put a live goldfish in it—instead of a cherry or olive or such things that occur to a commonplace mind.

You gulp.

The sensation of enclosing a squirm is delightfully revolting.

> I think it's immoral. I have named it the Dreiser cocktail.[70]

Only this, about the publication of the book that was to change his life.

Chapter Four

Damned Things

There is a great deal, in the most acceptable of the science of today, that represents a rehabilitation of supposed legends, superstitions, and folk lore. Recall Voltaire's incredulity as to fossils, which according to him only a peasant would believe in. . . . Here was one of the keenest of minds: but it could not accept data, because it rejected explanations of the data. . . . There are some backward ones, today, who do not believe in witches: but every married man knows better.

Lo!

Man is the pattern-making animal. Seeing pictures in clouds, or in flames of an open fire, or in the grain of wood, or water spots on a wall, is one of the oldest of solitary pleasures. Fort often referred to this game in his fiction; he himself had played it more elaborately than most. "I covered sheets of paper with scrawls, to see what

I could visualize out of them; tacked a sheet of wrapping paper to a ceiling, smudged it with a candle flame; made what I called a 'visualizing curtain,' which was a white window shade, covered with clay."[71] This was in his novel-writing period; he had the notion that these visualizing apparatuses might help him see the characters in a novel and describe them more vividly. But he was working toward something else, something he had glimpsed in his boyhood.

> In days of yore, when I was an especially bad young one, my punishment was having to go to the store, Saturdays, and work. I had to scrape off labels of other dealers' canned goods, and paste on my parents' label. Theoretically, I was so forced to labor to teach me the errors of deceitful ways. A good many brats are brought up, in the straight and narrow, somewhat deviously.
>
> One time I had pyramids of canned goods, containing a variety of fruits and vegetables. But I had used all except peach labels. I pasted the peach labels on peach cans, and then came to apricots. Well, aren't apricots peaches? And there are plums that are virtually apricots. I went on, either mischievously, or scientifically, pasting the peach labels on cans of plums, cherries, string beans, and succotash. I can't quite define my motive, because to this day it has not been decided whether I am a humorist or a scientist.[72]

He was a skeptic, with a deep distrust of established categories. He knew that all categories are conventional, and that every system of categories excludes other systems which may be equally valid. He knew, too, that we can only see what we are looking for, and he was tantalized by the feeling that there are unsuspected patterns all around us, which would be visible if we only knew where and how to look.

For years he had collected occasional notes on what seemed to him to be unexplained phenomena. Now he began to collect them in earnest. He had arrived at the idea, which was the major achievement of his life, that if there are unsuspected patterns in the universe, they must be found precisely here, in the data that do not fit known patterns.

> A search for the unexplained became an obsession. I undertook the job of going through all scientific periodicals, at least by way of indexes, published in English and French, from the year 1880, available in the libraries of New York . . . As I went along, with my little suspicions in their infancies, new subjects appeared to me—something queer about some hailstorms —the odd and the unexplained in archaeological discoveries, and in Arctic explorations. By the time I got through with the "grand tour," as I called this search of all available periodicals, to distinguish it from special investigations, I was interested in so many subjects that had cropped up later, or that I had missed earlier, that I made the tour all over again—and then again had the same experience, and had to go touring again—and so on—until now it is my recognition that in every field of phenomena—and in later years I have multiplied

> my subjects by very much shifting to the newspapers—is somewhere the unexplained, or the irreconcilable, or the mysterious—in unformulable motions of all planets; volcanic eruptions, murders, hailstorms, protective colorations of insects, chemical reactions, disappearances of human beings, stars, comets, juries, diseases, cats, lampposts, newly married couples, cathode rays, hoaxes, impostures, wars, births, deaths.[73]

It is a commonplace that writers, when adolescent, are solitary and rebellious. Fort, having rejected parental authority more definitively than usual—or having had it reject him, as may be—seems to have gone on to question all authority, and ultimately to reject it. He wrote:

> What is a straight line? A straight line is the shortest distance between two points. Well, then, what is a shortest distance between two points? That is a straight line. According to the test of ages, the definition that a straight line is a straight line cannot be improved on.[74]

And:

> I shall be scientific about it. Said Sir Isaac Newton—or virtually said he—"If there is no change in the direction of a moving body, the direction of a moving body is not changed." "But," continued he, "if something be changed, it is changed as much as it is changed." . . . How do geologists determine the age of rocks? By the fossils in them. And how do they de-

termine the age of fossils? By the rocks they're in. Having started with the logic of Euclid, I go on with the wisdom of a Newton.[75]

As for Darwinism:

The fittest survive.
What is meant by the fittest?
Not the strongest; not the cleverest—
Weakness and stupidity everywhere survive.
There is no way of determining fitness except in that a thing does survive.
"Fitness," then, is only another name for "survival."
Darwinism:
That survivors survive.[76]

The man who begins by questioning Euclid, Newton, and Darwin has set his foot on a dangerous path. He may end by doubting Harlow Shapley.

From his rejection of Darwinism, and therefore of mechanical evolution—random mutation came later, but he would have rejected that too—came an intimation of orthogenesis, of goal-directed evolution. He began to conceive of the universe as an organism, perhaps a fertilized egg, with roving corpuscles, capillary flows of nutrients. He noted the many instances in which things that had been disastrously lacking were supplied: insects in Great Britain in 1869, for example; but he also noted instances in which the thing supplied was not in demand. ("If the gods send worms, that would be kind, if we were robins."[77]) And he noted instances in which the thing that was wanted was supplied, but in calamitous quantity. For example, during the drought in China, in 1889:

> Down upon monstrous need came relief that was enormous. At Hongkong, houses collapsed under a smash of alleviation. A fury of mercy tore up almost every street in the Colony. The people had prayed for rain. They got it. . . . At Canton, every pietist proclaimed the efficacy of prayer, and I think he was right about that: but the problem is to tone down all this efficacy.[78]

As he went on, he became the defender, not of any eccentric view of his own, but of the discarded data themselves. He was not opposed to science, or the scientific method, but to the closed system of this science or that, the elevation of hypothesis to dogma. He was opposed to stupidity, incompetence, selective blindness and other forms of intellectual dishonesty wherever he found them. He rescued the data, collected them, and let them speak for themselves.

Out of this labor came *The Book of the Damned*, published by Boni & Liveright in the spring of 1919.

> A procession of the damned.
>
> By the damned, I mean the excluded.
>
> We shall have a procession of data that Science has excluded.
>
> Battalions of the accursed, captained by pallid data that I have exhumed, will march. You'll read them—or they'll march. Some of them livid and some of them fiery and some of them rotten.
>
> Some of them are corpses, skeletons, mummies, twitching, tottering, animated by companions that have been damned alive. There are

giants that will walk by, though sound asleep. There are things that are theorems and things that are rags: they'll go by like Euclid arm in arm with the spirit of anarchy. Here and there will flit little harlots. Many are clowns. But many are of the highest respectability. Some are assassins. There are pale stenches and gaunt superstitions and mere shadows and lively malices: whims and amiabilities. The naive and the pedantic and the bizarre and the grotesque and the sincere and the insincere, the profound and the puerile.

A stab and a laugh and the patiently folded hands of hopeless propriety. . . .

The power that has said to all these things that they are damned, is Dogmatic Science.

But they'll march.

The little harlots will caper, and freaks will distract attention, and the clowns will break the rhythm of the whole with their buffooneries—but the solidity of the procession as a whole: the impressiveness of things that pass and pass and pass, and keep on and keep on and keep on coming.

The irresistibleness of things that neither threaten nor jeer nor defy, but arrange themselves in mass-formations that pass and pass and keep on passing.[79]

The response from men of letters was immediate and enthusiastic. Booth Tarkington wrote to *The Bookman:* "Who in the name of frenzy is Charles Fort? . . . I'm just pulling up from influenza and this blamed book kept me all night when I certainly should have slept— . . . People must turn to look at his head as he walks down the street; I think it's a head that would emit noises and explosions, with copper flames playing out from the ears." Later, in the introduction he wrote for *New Lands,* he said: "Here indeed was a 'brush dipped in earthquake and eclipse'; though the wildest mundane earthquakes are but earthquakes in teapots compared to what goes on in the visions conjured up before us by Mr. Charles Fort."[80]

John Cowper Powys wrote: "I am indeed struck sharply and starkly by the curious genius of Mr. Charles Fort; and here in the 'Times' of yesterday or today comes on the front page an allusion to one of those 'red rains.' . . ."

Ben Hecht, reviewing *The Book of the Damned* in the Chicago *Daily News,* said: "I am the first disciple of Charles Fort. He has made a terrible onslaught upon the accumulated lunacy of fifty centuries. The onslaught will perish. The lunacy will survive, entrenching itself behind the derisive laughter of all good citizens. I, however, for one, rush to surrender my homage. Whatever the purpose of Charles Fort, he has delighted me beyond all men who have written books in this world. Mountebank or Messiah, it matters not. Henceforth I am a Fortean. If it has pleased Charles Fort to perpetrate a Gargantuan jest upon unsuspecting readers, all the better. If he has in all seriousness heralded forth the innermost truths of his soul, well and good. I offer him this testament. I believe."[81]

The Book of the Damned, Fort said, is "an assemblage of data of external relations of this earth. We take the position that our data have been damned, upon no consideration for individual merits or demerits, but in conformity with a general attempt to hold out for isolation of this earth."[82]

In the eighteenth century, for example, it was agreed

that stones do not fall from the sky, because there are no stones in the sky. Therefore people who thought they had seen stones fall from the sky were mistaken. Lightning might occasionally strike a stone and heat it; but the stone had been there in the first place; or, on occasion, a whirlwind might pick up stones from one location and deposit them in another.

Just so, to this day, conventionalists have explained away all falls of things that are not meteorites. The classic case is the one Fort later gave in the first chapter of *Lo!* On May 28, 1881, in Worcester, England, during a violent thunderstorm, tons of periwinkles fell from the sky, covering fields and a road for a distance of about a mile. Hermit crabs, and small crabs of an unidentified species, also fell. It was said that periwinkles had been seen along the roadside before the storm, and that probably a fishmonger had dumped them there.

> If a red-hot stove should drop from a cloud into Broadway, someone would find that at about the time of the occurrence, a moving van had passed, and that the moving men had tired of the stove, or something—that it had not been really red-hot, but had been rouged instead of blacked, by some absentminded housekeeper. Compared with some of the scientific explanations that we have encountered, there's considerable restraint, I think, in that one.[83]

Fall after fall after fall. And the explanations: "There in the first place." "Up from one place, down in another." As for whirlwinds, Fort wrote:

> Coffins have come down from the sky: also, as everybody knows, silk hats and horse collars and

> pajamas. . . . The two statements that I start with are that no shower exclusively of coffins, nor of marriage certificates, nor of alarm clocks has been recorded: but that showers exclusively of living things are common. . . . The explanation is that little frogs, for instance, fall from the sky, unmixed with anything else, because, in a whirlwind, the creatures were segregated by differences in specific gravity. But when a whirlwind strikes a town, away go detachables in a monstrous mixture, and there's no findable record of washtubs coming down in one place, all the town's cats in one falling battle that lumps its infelicities in one place, and all the kittens coming down together somewhere else, in a distant bunch that miaows for its lump of mothers.[84]

Thus, unless we believe in God or fishmongers, we have two problems: the origin of these things that fall from the sky, and their segregation. To these we must add a third, their repetition.

> There is an account, in the London Daily News, Sept. 5, 1922, of little toads, which for two days had been dropping from the sky, at Chalon-sur-Saône, France.[85]

And:

> *Year Book of Facts,* 1861-273:
> Quotation from a letter from Prof. Campini to Prof. Matteucci:
> That, upon Dec. 28, 1860, at about 7 A.M., in

the northwestern part of Siena, a reddish rain fell copiously for two hours.

A second red shower fell at 11 o'clock.

Three days later, the red rain fell again.

The next day another red rain fell.

Still more extraordinarily:

Each fall occurred in "exactly the same quarter of town."[86]

Things that pass and pass and keep on passing. . . . Camille Flammarion, in *The Atmosphere,* lists many showers of blood in Europe from ancient times to the nineteenth century. In 1571, for example, "there fell near Einden, during the night, so much blood that over a space of five or six miles the grass and clothes exposed had assumed a dark purple hue. Many persons preserved some of it in vessels. It was attempted, but unsuccessfully, to show that this prodigy was due to the rising into the air of the vapor from the blood of oxen that had been killed. No other explanation was found more deserving of credit among natural causes."

In 1744 red rain fell in San Pier d'Arena, near Genoa, "which, on account of the war then going on in the territory of the Republic, terrified the inhabitants very much; but it was subsequently ascertained that this tint was due to some red earth which a strong wind had carried into the air from a neighboring mountain." The name of the scientist who ascertained this is lost. Flammarion quotes G. Schott, on red rains in general: "What the vulgar call a shower of blood is generally a mere fall of vapors tinted with vermilion or red chalk. But when blood actually does fall, which it would be difficult to deny takes place, it is a miracle due to the will of God."

Another red rainfall is charmingly explained in the

same chapter. In July, 1608, "one of these pretended showers of blood fell in the outskirts of Aix (Provence), and this shower extended to the distance of half a league from the town. Some priests, either being themselves deceived or wishing to work upon the credulity of the people, at once attributed it to diabolic influence. Fortunately, a person of education, M. de Peiresc, examined very minutely into this apparent prodigy, studying in particular some drops that fell upon the wall of the cemetery attached to the principal church in Aix. He soon discovered that they were in reality the excrements of some butterflies which had been noticed in large numbers during the early part of July. There were no spots of the kind in the centre of the town, where the butterflies had not made their appearance, and, moreover, none were noticed upon the higher parts of the houses, above the level to which they flew. Besides, the presence of these drops in places protected from the air rendered it impossible that they could have their origin in the atmosphere. He at once pointed this out to those who regarded the occurrence as miraculous; but, in despite of the proofs which he adduced, the inhabitants persisted in attributing these drops to a supernatural cause."[87]

In the autumn of 1846 there was a fall of reddish substance in the south of France, accompanied by lightning, cloudbursts, hurricanes, etc. C. G. Ehrenberg, who analyzed samples of this substance, is said to have found in them "seventy-three organic formations, some of which were peculiar to Southern America." The force of the wind, says Flammarion, was so great that it was able "to detach a stratum of land in districts where the surface of the ground was sandy or of some other soft substance." The fall was thin in some places; "at Lyons, in fact, it was scarcely apparent, though it occurred in the shape of a reddish slime which was popularly converted into a *shower of blood.* But at Meximieux a battalion of soldiers marching toward the Swiss frontier were covered with the mud, and their uniforms impregnated with it. The Château de Chamagnieu was bespattered in such a way that it could scarcely be recognized. . . ." The interval between the departure of this dirt from the New World and its arrival in France, according to Flammarion, was "about four days, which gives a speed of eighteen and three-quarter yards per second." The name of the scientist who calculated this interval has been forgotten.

Flammarion explains a fall of red snow in May, 1863, in the eastern Pyrenees, as being composed of "marshy and ferruginous clay, mixed up with fine sand, which, as it passed through the atmosphere, deprived it of a portion of the organic matters in suspension there. In this way these rains serve a fertilizing purpose, being in fact *showers of manure.*"[88]

He also cites numerous reports of falls of nutritious substances. In 1824 and again in 1828, in one of the districts of Persia, a substance of this kind fell in "so abundant a shower . . . that it covered the ground to the depth of five or six inches. It was a kind of lichen, of a sort already known; cattle and sheep devoured it greedily, and some bread was even made from it." He quotes a statement by Johnston that in Carinthia, over a tract of land two miles long, there fell a shower of wheat, "with which bread was afterward made."

He is dubious about reports of falls of mineral sulfur, but considers falls of pollen, flowers, leaves, etc., well authenticated. He mentions a fall of dried oak leaves at Autrèche (Indre et Loire), April 9, 1869. "This phenomenon," he says, "seems to have resulted from a great squall which occurred on April 3; the oak leaves carried up by a hurricane into the higher regions of the atmosphere were kept there by the wind for six days, and fell again when the weather became calm."[89]

Fort refers to this passage in *The Book of the Damned,* and points out what he calls "Flammarion's two incredibilities . . . that leaves could remain a week in the air: that they could stay together a week in the air." He also calls attention to the fact that these were *dried* oak leaves, and that the fall occurred in April. He then cites two more falls of dried leaves, one at Clairvaux and Outre-Aube, France, on April 7, 1894, the other at Pontcarré four days later. These reports are from *L'Astronomie,* whose editor was Flammarion; and of course Flammarion explained. As Fort puts it: "He says that the leaves had been caught up in a cyclone which had expended its force; that the heavier leaves had fallen first. We think that that was all right for 1894, and that it was quite good enough for 1894. But, in these more exciting days, we want to know how wind-power insufficient to hold some leaves in the air could sustain others four days."

Then, after another paragraph, these three pregnant sentences:

> Inspiration:
> That there may be a nearby world complementary to this world, where autumn occurs at the time that is springtime here.
> Let some disciple have that.[90]

Here we can see exactly why Fort was driven to deny conventional astronomy in toto. Not only do things fall to this earth which can be traced to no earthly origin, but things—the same sort of things—fall repeatedly on the same spot. If this can happen, and if aerial explosions occur with earthquakes, and if these, too, occur again and again over the same spot on this earth, then there must be a fixed relation between the earth and some other body, and for other reasons it is clear that this body must be nearby.

Conventional astronomy says that the Earth is not fixed in relation to anything and that it is separated by vast distances from all other heavenly bodies. Therefore Fort was logically compelled to reject conventional astronomy. Sometimes he put a large question mark in its place; at other times, drawn out of his neutrality in spite of himself, he argued for a new cosmology; somewhere above the Earth, he said, there was a Super-Sargasso Sea.

> I think that things raised from this earth's surface to that region have been held there until shaken down by storms— . . .
>
> Derelicts, rubbish, old cargoes from inter-planetary wrecks; things cast out into what is called space by convulsions of other planets, things from the times of the Alexanders, Caesars and Napoleons of Mars and Jupiter and Neptune; things raised by this earth's cyclones: horses and barns and elephants and flies and dodoes, moas, and pterodactyls; leaves from modern trees and leaves of the Carboniferous era—all, however, tending to disintegrate into homogeneous-looking muds or dusts, red or black or yellow—treasure-troves for the palaeontologists and for the archeologists—accumulations of centuries—cyclones of Egypt, Greece, and Assyria—fishes dried

> hard, there a short time: others there long enough to putrify—[91]

At other times he spoke of vast superconstructions, navigable or adrift in interplanetary space. He gave them names: Monstrator; Elvera; Genesistrine; Azuria. He spoke of our puzzlement over things that fall down to us through the atmosphere, and asked us to imagine how deep-sea fish might feel, staring goggle-eyed at things that fall through their ocean, from unimaginable realms above. Or this, speaking of a fall of dust and red rain that occurred in Europe in 1903:

> I think, myself, that in 1903, we passed through the remains of a powdered world—left over from an ancient inter-planetary dispute, brooding in space like a red resentment ever since.[92]

Chapter Five

But They'll March

Although seemingly unpredictable, the progress of a science usually has three stages. First, some new means of experiment or observation is developed into a powerful tool. It provides a fresh look at nature. In the second, the proliferation of data may cause frustration and bewilderment, since the new results may not be understandable on the basis of known scientific principles. In general this stage lasts longest. But sooner or later final clarification comes, for someone develops a new concept that explains the baffling results naturally and in a straightforward manner.

Su-Shu Huang

In the reading room of the New York Public Library, that vast mausoleum, designed by some schoolmaster with memories of hard oak, dust and gloom, there are men who sit day after day, bulwarked by stacks of books, scribbling, scribbling in the little pools of light from the green-shaded lamps on the long oak tables, and you look at them and wonder what will-o'-the-wisps they are pursuing day after day, year after year. One of them may be writing a history of dentistry in America, another studying explosives in order to blow up the world, a third gathering evidence that Shakespeare wrote the Bible. Their faces are pale and grim. The only cheerful people in that place are those who do not read the books, but only handle them as they come from the dumbwaiter, and set them on the counter like moldy slabs of beef. Those who sit at the long tables day after day are dedicated men; some of them are brave men. There is death in old books from the stacks of a great library; the dust that impregnates their pages is death and darkness; the dust says, "These are books that no one has opened for twenty years, fifty years, eighty years; and when you have written your book, it too will gather dust." White book dust, bone dust: garden dirt and axle grease are clean in comparison; they are living and unctuous; rubbed into the skin, they do good. The dust of books causes blains and hangnails; ingested, it provokes dyspepsia, flatulence, and heartburn; in the lungs it is cancerous. Who would not choose, if he could, to sit chained to an oar in a Roman galley, in the sunlight and salt air, rather than in this sunless crypt where, in the years from 1905 to 1920, Charles Fort sat? Many people must have wondered why he was here behind his tall stack of books: but one does not ask. Perhaps there is another like him there today, silent and determined under the green-shaded lamp.

"We shall pick up an existence by its frogs," wrote Fort in a memorable phrase; but he also told of falls of alkali, asbestos, ashes, axes;

of beef, birds, bitumen, blood, brick, and butter;
of carbonate of soda, charcoal, cinders, coal, coffee beans, and coke;
of fibers, fish, flesh, and flints;
of gelatin, grain, and greenstone;
of hay;
of ice, insects, and iron;
of larvae, leaves, and lizards;
of manna;
of nostoc;
of sand, seeds, silk, snakes, soot, spiderwebs, stones, and sulfur;
of turpentine, and turtles;
of water, and worms.

In addition, he told of things seen in the sky; unknown objects observed in space; storms associated with earthquakes and volcanic eruptions; aerial detonations and darknesses; appearances and disappearances of living things, including human beings; poltergeist phenomena; mysterious assaults, stabbings, phantom bullets; fires that consumed people internally; asphyxiations; things seen in the ocean.

"I shall attempt not much of correlation of dates," said Fort. Nevertheless, many of his data were collected purely because they correlated with other data. By assiduous reading and comparison of newspapers and scientific journals, Fort discovered, for example, that storms and other aerial phenomena—meteors, electrical discharges, luminous appearances in the sky—occur at the time of earthquakes with a frequency which is implausible, unless there is some unsuspected relation between convulsions in the earth and those in the atmosphere.

Note these dates, all in late 1879 and early 1880:

October 10, 1879—a "cloudburst" in Jamaica. October 14, another in Murcia and Alicante provinces in Spain.

November 1, an earthquake in West Cumberland, England, accompanied by a "vivid flash" in the sky. December 19, a "cloudburst" in Colombia. On the following day, earthquakes in El Salvador, near Lake Ilopango, supposed to be the crater of an extinct volcano. On the thirty-first of December, more earthquakes near the lake. And—

> Water fell from the sky, in bulks that gouged gullies. Gullies writhed in the quaking ground. The inhabitants who cried to the heavens prayed to Epilepsy. Mud was falling upon the convulsions. A volcanic island was rising in Lake Ilopango, displacing the water, in streams that writhed from it violently.

On January 4, 1880, in the island of Dominica, British West Indies, "the town of Roseau was bumped by midnight. People in the streets were attacked by darkness. People in houses heard the smash of their window panes. Night fell so heavily that it broke roofs. It was a daytime night of falling mud. With the mud came a deluge. . . .

"In the Boiling Lakes District of Dominica, there had been an eruption of mud, at the time of the deluge. . . . There had, in recorded time, never been an eruption here before."

On January 12, a "waterspout" struck the island of St. Kitts, B.W.I.: a fist of water that carried away houses, drowned two hundred and fifty people. On the same day, water was falling on the island of Grenada, three hundred miles away, "as it had never rained before, in the history of the island." Fort sums up:

> Beginning upon October 10th, and continuing until the occurrence at St. Kitts, deluge after

> deluge came down to one zone around this earth —or a flight of lakes was cast from a constellational reservoir, which was revolving and discharging around a zone of this earth. . . .[93]

In 1883 and for years thereafter, there were extraordinary sunsets; also there were blue moons. Scientists explained that these were due to the enormous quantity of dust discharged into the upper atmosphere by the eruption of Krakatoa on August 28. This explanation has been repeated ever since, in textbooks and popular science books, and we have always found it comforting. But:

> *Annual Register*, 1883-105:
> That the atmospheric effects that have been attributed to Krakatoa were seen in Trinidad before the eruption occurred;
> *Knowledge*, 5-418:
> That they were seen in Natal, South Africa, six months before the eruption.[94]

Fort also notes that the atmospheric effects continued for seven years after Krakatoa. "Except that, in the seven, there was a lapse of several years—and where was the volcanic dust all that time?"[95]

Falls of coke and pebbles and fish. . . . And again and again, the notation: "in a heavy storm"; "with hail"; "in a thunderstorm."

Then the aerial explosions, recorded over a period of centuries, at Comrie, Scotland; or the similar explosions, the "Barisal guns," heard in triplets, sometimes as many as thirty or forty a day, for years at Barisal, India. Or the black rains of Slains, Scotland. . . .

Or the unaccountable darkness that overwhelmed Canada and parts of the northern United States on November 19, 1819. A black rain fell, and there were earthquakes. Fort wrote that "it will soon be our expression that profound darkness, fall of matter from the sky, lights in the sky, and earthquakes are phenomena of the near approach of other worlds to this world."[96]

The "light-wheel" phenomenon is one of the most curious and suggestive things in Fort. The following account is typical; it was written by J. W. Robertson, who in 1880 was aboard the British India Company steamer *Patna,* in the Persian Gulf.

> In May, 1880, on a dark night, about 11:30 P.M., there suddenly appeared on each side of the ship an enormous luminous wheel, whirling around, the spokes of which seemed to brush the ship along. The spokes would be 200 or 300 yards long, and resembled the birch rods of the dames' schools. Each wheel contained about sixteen spokes, and, although the wheels must have been some 500 or 600 yards in diameter, the spokes could be distinctly seen all the way round. The phosphorescent gleam seemed to glide along flat on the surface of the sea, no light being visible in the air above the water. The appearance of the spokes could be almost exactly represented by standing in a boat and flashing a bull's eye lantern horizontally along the surface of the water, round and round. I may mention that the phenomenon was also seen by Captain Avern, of the *Patna,* and Mr. Manning, third officer.[97]

Fort lists ten independent reports of the same phenomenon between 1848 and 1910, all but one in the Gulf of Persia. Among those who saw the wheels were Captain Hoseason of the steamship *Kilwa,* R. E. Harris, Commander of the A.H.N. Company steamship *Shahjehan,* S. C. Patterson, second officer of the P. & O. steamship *Delta,* Commander J. E. Pringle of H.M.S. *Vulture,* Captain Gabe of the Danish East Asiatic Company steamship *Bintang,* and Captain Breyer of the Dutch steamer *Valentijn.* The light was not phosphorescence; it seemed to be coming from beneath the surface of the water.

Fort adds several observations of things seen plunging into the ocean or emerging from it. It is tantalizing to think that there may have been—may still be—vast illuminated constructions in the ocean where we can't get at them: vehicles from another world, perhaps a watery world; so that when they arrive, instead of asking to be taken to our leader, they head directly for the only portion of our globe that is of any use to them, the ocean.

Perhaps they consider it *their* ocean. As I write these lines, the papers are full of stories about the disappearance of the nuclear-powered United States attack submarine *Scorpion* on May 27, 1968. I remember the Israeli sub *Dakar* and the French *Minerve;* and I am reminded of some notes Thayer published in *Doubt,* of four submarines that sank or disappeared between February and June, in 1939: the Japanese *I-63,* the United States *Squalus,* the British *Thetis,* and the French *Phenix.*

Fort's data do not submit tamely to classification. I have a column labeled for convenience "Things seen in the sky," which includes all sorts of things, from mirages to glares. I have no reason to think they are all logically connected; on the other hand, I don't know that they are not. In they go, in a lump. I have a column labeled "Assaults," and another labeled "Epidemics," meaning outbreaks of various kinds of unusual human behavior; but some of the epidemics are assaults. The compartments leak. Here are poltergeist phenomena: things thrown about by invisible forces, mysterious fires in wallpaper, raps and explosive sounds, stones falling from appearing points under ceilings. Typically, all these things happen inside a single house. But there are many other cases in which stones fall on roofs of houses. Sometimes other things fall on roofs. On the twelfth and thirteenth of October, 1888, a lighthouse at Point Isabel, Texas, was pelted with nails, clods, and oyster shells.

No one is ever seen throwing these things, although police and neighbors always search. Sometimes the things fall from such heights that catapults are thought of, but never found. A frequent report is that stones, both inside and outside houses, fall with unnatural slowness. Some are warm to the touch, some cold. Sometimes water drips from appearing points under ceilings—the ceilings remaining dry—and is collected in buckets.

And water drips from the sky, sometimes, in a tiny fixed area, again and again over a period of days—falling on a single tree.

Fires break out in wallpaper, during poltergeist occurrences. Sometimes, on these occasions, the fires occur on the backs of women's dresses. And sometimes fires occur inside the bodies of human beings. Fort has thirteen examples of this. The victim, usually an old woman, but occasionally an old man, is found almost completely consumed by a fire which has only scorched nearby furniture and walls. Frequently a greasy residue is found deposited on walls. The victim is usually seated in a chair, and almost always alone in a closed house. In England, from December, 1904, to March, 1905, there were six such occurrences. The most recent that I know of was in 1959, in Pontiac, Michigan.

I have some of Fort's data in a separate file, not indexed with the rest; these are things that can't be dated. A nail, for example, found in a block of stone taken from the Kingoodie Quarry in Great Britain. Another, found in a chunk of auriferous quartz in California. "Pygmy flints," worked stone implements, some only a quarter-inch long, found in Europe, India, South Africa. "So fine is the chipping that to see the workmanship a magnifying glass is necessary."[98] A stone ax, 28″×14″ ×11″, found in Birchwood, Wisconsin. It weighed 300 pounds. A copper ax, 22 inches long, weighing 38 pounds, taken from a burial mound in Ohio.

Three other reports seem to form a suggestive pattern of their own, which extends somewhat more dubiously to others; I have these under "Multiple deaths," but I have tagged them "Asphyxiation." Three men found dead on Sand Island, in the Caspian Sea, sometime before January, 1909: no sign of struggle or injury. Autopsies showed no poison. "The doctors, though they would not commit themselves to an explanation, thought the men had been stifled." Then in 1925, four mountain climbers, three of whom died, in the Tatra Mountains in Poland. The survivor, a woman, said they had dropped unconscious one by one. She said it was "a stifling wind."[99]

I think of unbreathable atmospheres of other planets —odorless methane, maybe, or just an oxygen atmosphere with too much nitrogen or carbon dioxide in it—dropping like invisible smoke through an appearing point above the ground.

Then there was the wedding party in Bradford, England, in March, 1923. People screamed, dropped unconscious; four were taken to hospitals. Mass hysteria, perhaps: but people in adjoining houses also dropped unconscious. And what about the "miasma" that caused scores of people to fall unconscious in the streets of El Paso in 1929? The year after that a "lethal fog" killed seventy-seven people in the Meuse valley in Belgium. There were mutterings about the poison gas used in World War I, twelve years before.

From February to April, 1968, a "mysterious gas" on Wake Island sent as many as sixty people a day to the island dispensary, and caused officials to declare parts of the island off limits. The area manager, George Lacaille, said he believed the gas might be coming from "gas-filled cylinders that the Japanese are known to have had when they occupied the atoll from December, 1941, to 1945." I note that when ghosts walk, in the South Pacific, they are usually said to be victims of the Japanese who occupied the islands in World War II. It is also said that American officials are less superstitious than the natives of the South Pacific. Fort would have urged us to keep an open mind about this.

Chapter Six

Vanishing Satellites

". . . when *I* find a thing," said the Duck, "it's usually a frog or a worm."

Alice's Adventures in Wonderland

From 1645 to 1764 fifteen astronomers reported observing a satellite of Venus. Cassini, the discoverer of four of Saturn's moons, saw it; James Short, the mathematician and instrument-maker, saw it; Tobias Mayer saw it. Following the observations of Montaigne in 1761, the German mathematician Johann Lambert calculated its orbit, giving it a mean distance from Venus of 259,000 miles, a period of eleven days five hours, and an orbital eccentricity of 0.195. After March, 1764, nobody saw it again, and modern astronomers conclude that it was never there at all. As Patrick Moore puts it, in *The Planet Venus:* "Satellites do not 'softly and silently vanish away,' like the hunters of the Snark. . . ."

If it was never there, how could fifteen astronomers, over a period of more than a century, have been convinced that they saw it?

Moore explains:

> The problem was more or less cleared up in 1887 by Dr. Paul Stroobant, of Brussels, who published an elaborate memoir in which he reprinted all the observations . . . and subjected them to a critical analysis. Some, such as Scheuten's, could be rejected outright, since the 1761 transit was watched by many observers with better telescopes than his, and nobody else had seen a trace of the companion. Others, such as Montaigne's, could be due only to "ghost reflections," while still others could be put down to the observations of small stars. Horrebow, for instance, seems to have seen the fifth-magnitude star Theta Librae, while it is possible that what Roedkiaer saw was the then unknown planet Uranus.[100]

That takes care of Horrebow and Roedkiaer, but what about the rest?

Moore goes on to discuss "ghost reflections." Then he says: "Admittedly, it is strange to understand how such skillful observers as Cassini and Short fell into an elementary trap, but since the satellite is obviously nonexistent there is no alternative."[101]

Moore's reasoning might be summarized as follows: There is no satellite of Venus now. Therefore there could have been no satellite of Venus in 1645–1764. Therefore the observers who said they saw it must have been mistaken.

"Eliminate the impossible," said Conan Doyle's Sherlock Holmes. "Whatever remains, however improbable, must be true."

In order to admit that Cassini, Montaigne, and Short were deceived by "ghost reflections," we must believe that these experienced observers neglected the elementary test of turning the eyepiece.

Note these passages, from Moore's own account:

> Short recorded that when he first glimpsed the satellite, seeing was so good that two of the dusky shadings were visible on Venus' disk. The diameter of the attendant was about 1/3 that of Venus, and although not brilliant it was exceedingly sharp and well-defined. *It was seen with three separate eyepieces (giving magnifications of 60, 140 and 240) and even with a second telescope. . . .*
>
> Montaigne first saw the satellite on 3rd May 1761, and described it as a little crescent-shaped body about 22 minutes of arc away from Venus. As usual, it showed the same phase as the planet itself, and had one-quarter the diameter of Venus, which agreed well with the description left by Cassini. Montaigne repeated the observation several times during the night, and on May 4th, 7th and 11th (the intervening nights were cloudy) he saw the companion again, differently placed but still showing the same phase. . . . Montaigne, who had hitherto been decidedly sceptical about the real existence of the satellite, was convinced. He stated that he had taken every possible precaution against optical illusion, *and that he had seen the companion even when*

Venus itself was put outside the field of view.[102] (Italics mine.)

A temporary satellite of Venus is improbable. "Ghost reflections," under the described conditions, are impossible.

From 1762 onwards, for more than a century, astronomers reported observations of an infra-Mercurian planet. In 1859 Leverrier, the discoverer of Neptune, announced that from six such observations he had calculated the orbit of the planet. He adopted the name "Vulcan," given to this hypothetical body by the Abbe Moigno. He placed the time of best observation at March 22, 1877. When that day came, there was no Vulcan. It is now said that there never was such a body.

It had been seen by Standacher, Lichtenberg, Hoffman, Dangos, Stark, Hind, Scott, Wray, Lowe, Russell, De Vico, Coumbray, Fritsche, De Cuppis, Sidebotham, Lescarbault, Lummis, Denning, Schmidt, Lofft, Steinheibel, and Wolf. The last of these observations was in 1876.

Fort remarks that Leverrier, who had already announced the probable existence of an infra-Mercurian planet, chose six observations that agreed with his calculations, and disregarded the rest. If more than twenty astronomers saw what they said they saw, and if only six of these observations agreed with Leverrier's calculated orbit, the most obvious conclusion is that there was more than one "Vulcan."

In 1878, a year after the failure of Leverrier's prediction, "two shining objects at a considerable distance from the sun" were observed independently by Swift in Denver and Watson in Wyoming, during the total eclipse of July 29. In *Nature*, August 20, 1878, Lockyer wrote: "There is little doubt that an Infra-Mercurial planet has been discovered by Prof. Watson."

In 1921, at Mount Hamilton, "an unknown luminous object . . . near the sun"[103] was seen by Professor Campbell. A visiting aviator, Captain Eddie Rickenbacker, also saw it.

Fort gives dozens of other observations of unknown objects seen near the Sun or crossing its disk. Some are damned things, indeed. A "vast, spindle-shaped body, about three of the sun's digits in breadth and nine in length," was observed independently on August 9, 1762, by de Rostan in Basle, France, and Croste in Sole, Switzerland. The *Annual Register* remarked: "In a word, we know of nothing to have recourse to, in the heavens, by which to explain this phenomenon."[104]

In August, 1877, Asaph Hall discovered the two moons of Mars. They had not been seen before, although other astronomers, including Herschel, had searched for them diligently.

Four of Jupiter's satellites were discovered by Galileo in 1610. Eight of Saturn's nine satellites were discovered before 1849. Two of Uranus's satellites were discovered by Herschel in 1787. One of Neptune's two satellites was discovered by Lassell in 1846, only a few weeks after the planet itself was found.

Herschel, in the years 1790–1798, continued to search for more satellites of Uranus, *and thought he had found four more.* "He expresses so much confidence as to the real existence of these four bodies that it is very difficult for those who appreciate his skill to understand how he could have been deceived. But he admits that he was unable to watch any of these satellites through a considerable part of its path, or to identify any of them on different nights. All he felt sure about was that certain points of light were seen which did not remain stationary, as would have happened had they been fixed stars."[105] Other satellites of Uranus have since been discovered, but they are much closer to the primary. The four bodies Herschel saw have never been found again.

The orbital distances and periods of the two moons of Mars are unusual. The inner moon, Phobos, orbits the planet in less than one-third the time of the primary's rotation; this makes it, as Hall pointed out, unique in the solar system. Deimos, the outer moon, has a period of thirty hours eighteen minutes, only about five and a half hours greater than that of the planet. "It almost behaves like an artificial synchronous satellite."[106] It has been suggested, by the Russian astronomer I. Shklovsky among others, that both Phobos and Deimos are in fact artificial satellites, put into orbit sometime between 1870 and 1875.

Hall's successor at the Washington Observatory, E. Holden, saw what he thought was a *third* satellite of Mars. "It was reserved for an American, Mr. E. Holden, to discover with the splendid refractor of the Washington Observatory an imaginary third satellite of Mars moving in direct disobedience to the law (Kepler's Third Law) which harmonizes all the celestial motions. But astronomers do not recognize this body."[107]

The earliest record of the appearance of a flying saucer, unless it is Ezekiel's, must be the following account by Gervase of Tilbury, who lived in the time of Henry II. I take this from a letter to a British newspaper in the twenties, found among the Fortean material in the Dreiser collection at the University of Pennsylvania.

One Sunday, the people of a village in Kent were coming out of church on a thick, cloudy day, when they saw the anchor of a ship hooked to one of the tombstones; the cable, which was highly stretched, hanging down from the air; the villagers were much astonished, and while they were consulting about it, suddenly they saw the rope move as though someone laboured to pull up the anchor.

The anchor, however, held still fast by the stone. Presently a sailor was seen sliding down the cable for the purpose of unfixing the anchor, and when he had just loosened it, the villagers seized hold of him, and while in their hands, he quickly died, just as though he had been drowned. In memory of this extraordinary event, the people of the village made the hinges of their church door out of the iron of the anchor, and there they are still to be seen.

I am not sure about this one myself, or about any of the other purported sightings of UFOs from which passengers emerged, whether they were little men in white armor, as in several modern tales, or men of normal size in fur coats, as in one account mentioned by Fort. But the number of UFO sightings by credible observers since 1952 is so large that I think it takes an admirable rigidity of intellect to dismiss them all as fantasy.

Most people suppose that the "saucer invasion" began in 1945, when Kenneth Arnold saw a chain of saucer-shaped objects flying over the Cascades in Washington. But the reports of these objects listed in *The Books of Charles Fort* go back to 1779.

Writers about UFOs, both pro and con, frequently

refer to a fixed percentage of UFO sightings which cannot be explained. Some writers say it is 2 percent, some 6 percent. This percentage is used, according to the writer's bias, to support the conclusion that there really are UFOs or that there are not. The curious thing is that, according to figures released by the Air Force Project Blue Book, no such fixed percentage exists. (See Figure 1.) Although the number of reported sightings varies widely from 1947 to 1967, the last year of record,[108] the number of *unidentified* sightings is almost level, and very small—the yearly average is just under twenty. The one exception is the year 1952, when reported sightings reached their highest peak—1,501—and unidentified sightings also peaked at 303, more than ten times the number for any other year. With this one exception, there is little or no correlation between the number of sightings and the number recorded as "unidentified."

If "unidentified" sightings are merely those which can be, but have not been, explained by conventional means, we would expect them to correlate positively with the total number of sightings: the number should go up when the total number goes up, down when it goes down. The absence of any such relationship from 1953 on is very curious and interesting. If these figures mean anything, which is by no means certain, there are "real" UFO sightings, which occur at a relatively low rate that has nothing to do with the fluctuations in spurious sightings. In 1952, however, the number of "real" sightings jumped from an average of twenty to more than three hundred, at the same time that spurious sightings jumped to twelve hundred.

An alternative explanation, which is perhaps too cynical, is that Project Blue Book's evaluation procedures

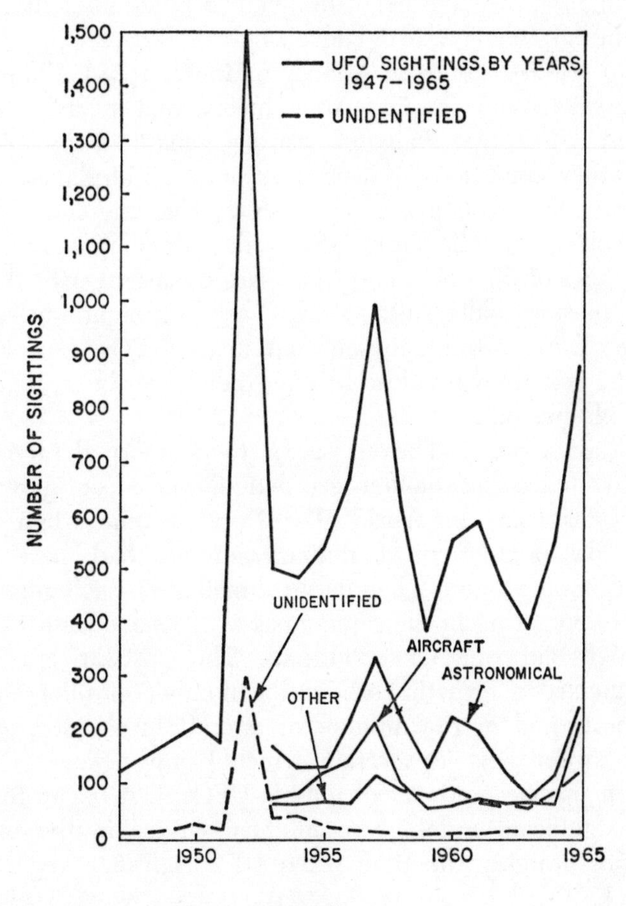

FIGURE 1

This chart shows the number of UFO sightings reported by Project Blue Book from 1947 to 1965. The breakdown into "Aircraft," "Astronomical" and "Other" has been made only since 1953.

from 1953 on have been designed to hold "unidentified" sightings to a low fixed level.

In *UFOs–Identified* (Random House, 1968), Philip J. Klass expounds an ingenious theory that many if not most UFOs are balls of plasma generated by freak weather conditions, power lines, and jet airplanes. His arguments are convincing; he shows that the colors and the observed behavior of UFOs—the sudden accelerations, changes of direction, and so on—are consistent with those of plasma balls, also known as ball lightning and *Kugelblitz.* I think myself that many UFOs, especially those seen moving close to the ground, can be explained as plasma balls.

Klass writes: "Thus it seems to be more than mere coincidence that the first recorded pilot reports of glowing fireballs came in World War II, at a time when the world's population of military aircraft had suddenly mushroomed and when large armadas of such aircraft were operating in the same areas at the same time, often under bad weather conditions. The postwar era has witnessed a growth both in the number of pilot UFO reports and in the number of aircraft in the sky. And the swept-wing jet aircraft, which I now believe is the most prolific producer of plasma-UFOs, first began to fly in significant numbers in military service in the early 1950s—roughly the time when UFO sightings began to peak."[109]

Alas, jet aircraft cannot account for that single sharp peak in unexplained sightings in 1952; the number of swept-wing jets in service has increased steadily since that date.

In its breakdown of sighting reports for 1966, Project Blue Book lists "plasma" only as a footnote (1 case); in its breakdown for 1967, "ionized air plasma" is listed, again as a footnote (1 case), and so is "ball lightning" (1 case). Most of the identified cases go into one of three categories—"Astronomical" (meteors, stars and planets), "Aircraft," and "Other," which includes hoaxes and hallucinations, missiles and rockets, reflections, flares and fireworks, mirages and inversions, search and groundlights, clouds and contrails, chaff, birds, and so on. It is not doubted by even the most dedicated UFOlogists that most UFO sightings can be put into these categories; but there are sightings that can be accounted for by none of them.[110]

Many of Fort's data concern things seen in the sky which were simply brilliant lights, fixed or moving: these could well have been bolides, plasma balls, or what you like. Others concern things seen which were not points or spheres of light: they were constructions. Excluding objects seen through telescopes, because of a doubt whether they were in our atmosphere or not, the first such observation is this one, paraphrased by Fort from the *Transactions* of the Swedish Academy of Science, 1808:

> That, upon the 16th of May, 1808, at about 4 P.M., the sun suddenly turned dull brick-red. At the same time there appeared, upon the western horizon, a great number of round bodies, dark brown, and seemingly the size of a hat crown. They passed overhead and disappeared in the eastern horizon. Tremendous procession. It lasted two hours. Occasionally one fell to the ground. When the place of a fall was examined, there was found a film, which soon dried and vanished. Often, when approaching the sun, these bodies seemed to link together, or were then seen to be linked together,

> in groups not exceeding eight, and, under the sun, they were seen to have tails three or four fathoms long. Away from the sun the tails were invisible. Whatever their substance may have been, it is described as gelatinous—"soapy and jellied."[111]

In 1882, at the Royal Observatory at Greenwich, E. W. Maunder saw "a strange celestial visitor." He described it later in *Observatory*.

> . . . Maunder was at the Royal Observatory, Greenwich, Nov. 17, 1882, at night. There was an aurora, without features of special interest. In the midst of the aurora, a great circular disk of greenish light appeared and moved smoothly across the sky. But the circularity was evidently the effect of foreshortening. The thing passed above the moon, and was, by other observers, described as "cigar-shaped," "like a torpedo," "a spindle," "a shuttle." The idea of foreshortening is not mine: Maunder says this. He says: "Had the incident occurred a third of a century later, beyond doubt everyone would have selected the same simile—it would have been 'just like a Zeppelin.'" The duration was about two minutes. Color said to have been the same as that of the auroral glow in the north. Nevertheless, Maunder says that this thing had no relation to auroral phenomena. "It appeared to be a definite body." Motion too fast for a cloud, but "nothing could be more unlike the rush of a meteor."[112]

In 1907 a torpedo-shaped construction was seen in the sky over Burlington, Vermont. Bishop John S. Michaud wrote this account of it for the *Monthly Weather Review:*

> "I was standing on the corner of Church and College Streets, just in front of the Howard Bank, and facing east, engaged in conversation with Ex-Governor Woodbury and Mr. A. A. Buell, when, without the slightest indication, or warning, we were startled by what sounded like a most unusual and terrific explosion, evidently very nearby. Raising my eyes, and looking eastward along College Street, I observed a torpedo-shaped body, some 300 feet away, stationary in appearance, and suspended in the air, about 50 feet above the tops of the buildings. In size it was about 6 feet long by 8 inches in diameter, the shell, or covering, having a dark appearance, with here and there tongues of fire issuing from spots on the surface, resembling red-hot, unburnished copper. Although stationary when first noticed, this object soon began to move, rather slowly, and disappeared over Dolan Brothers' store, southward. As it moved, the covering seemed rupturing in places, and through these the intensely red flames issued."[113]

In January, 1913, an "unknown airship" was seen over Dover, heading from the sea. This was on the fourth. On the seventeenth, Captain Lindsay, Chief Constable of Glamorganshire, saw a large object in the sky over Cardiff, Wales. "It was much larger than the Willows airship, and left in its trail a dense smoke. It disappeared quickly." A meteor, perhaps. But on the following day, people in Cardiff saw a lighted object in the sky. An airship carrying a brilliant light was seen over Liverpool. Similar reports came from Newport, Neath, and other places in Wales.

> In the [London] *Standard,* January 31, is published a list of cities where the object had been seen. Here a writer tries to conclude that some foreign airship had made half a dozen visits to England and Wales, or had come once, remaining three weeks; but he gives up the attempt, thinking that nothing could have reached England and have sailed away half a dozen times without being seen to cross the coast; thinking that the idea of anything having made one journey, and remaining three weeks in the air deserved no consideration.

The object carried a brilliant searchlight. "Streets and houses in the locality of Totterdown [Wales] were suddenly illuminated by a brilliant, piercing light, which, sweeping upward, gave many spectators a fine view of the hills beyond."[114]

On February 9 occurred an aerial spectacle that was seen in Canada, the United States, at sea, and in Bermuda. A group of luminous bodies with tails moved across the sky with "a peculiar, majestic deliberation." Another group followed, and then another.

"There were probably 30 or 32 bodies, and the peculiar thing about them was their moving in fours and threes and twos, abreast of one another; and so perfect was the lining up that you would have thought it was an aerial fleet maneuvering after rigid drilling."[115]

If they were meteors, says Fort, at least it will have to be admitted that they were like no meteors ever seen before. On the following day, in the sky over Toronto, another procession: this time the objects were dark. "They passed from west to east, in three groups, and then returned west in more scattered formation, about seven or eight in all."[116]

On February 21 the reports resumed in Great Britain. A luminous object was seen in the sky of Yorkshire and Warwickshire, and also over Ipswich; these places are more than a hundred miles apart. It was seen again on the twenty-fourth and twenty-fifth. The last account Fort could find was another from Captain Lindsay in Cardiff, April 8, that he and other persons had seen an object carrying a brilliant light and moving sixty or seventy miles an hour.

> If German airships were maneuvering over England, without being seen either approaching or departing, appearing sometimes far inland in England without being seen to cross the well-guarded coasts, it was secret maneuvering, inasmuch as the accusation was denied in Germany (*Times*, February 26 and 27). It was then one of the most brilliantly proclaimed of secrets, or it was concealment under one of the most powerful searchlights ever seen.[117]

The reports of unknown flying objects collected by Fort bear little resemblance, as a rule, to the "flying saucer" stereotype. Some were simply moving lights in the sky, some torpedo-shaped, some triangular. Others were like nothing on Earth, but showed definite evidence of structure. There was the thing seen by the crew of the bark *Lady of the Lake* on March 22, 1870. "According to Captain Banner, it was a cloud of circular form, with an included semicircle divided into four parts, the central dividing shaft beginning at the center of the circle and extending far outward, and then curving backward."[118] His sketch of it was published in the *Journal* of the Royal Meteorological Society.

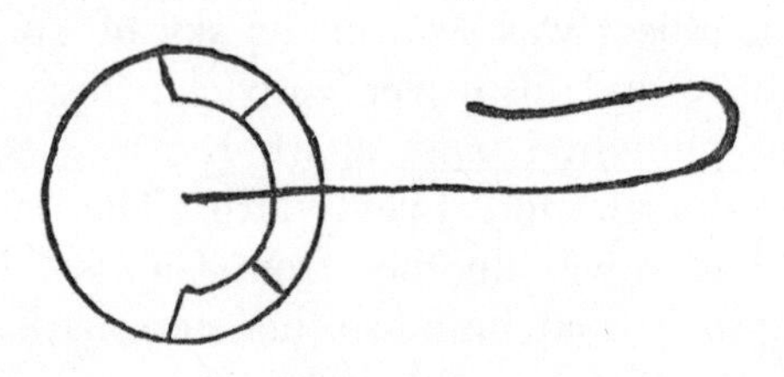

One salient fact about UFOs is missing from all modern accounts I have seen. Fort's data show that they are not isolated phenomena. Unknown flying objects, unknown bodies seen in space, appearances and disappearances, poltergeist activity, falls of strange substances and organisms from the sky—all these things show strong positive correlations with each other. Taken together, they show evidence of rhythmic fluctuation.

1. Raymond, Clarence and Charles.

2. John Hoy, Fort's maternal grandfather.

3. Peter V. Fort.

4. “They”: Charles Nelson Fort.

5. Agnes Fort.

6. Agnes and a friend.

7. Fort at 12.

8. Fort at 15.

9. Fort at 19.

10. Charles and Anna Fort—a passport photo.
(Courtesy of Aaron Sussman)

11. Charles Fort, c. 1920.
(Courtesy of Aaron Sussman)

2. 39 Marchmont Street, London, where Fort lived in the twenties. This photo was taken in 1955. Credit: Teddy Schwarz.

13. Fort at his super checkerboard.

14. Two covers of the magazine *Doubt* by the Fortean Society. The one on the left is a "spirit drawing showing Charles Fort on the Other Side. He has clearly dethroned the Hebrew Yaweh ('God' to you) and taken possession of Jupiter's thunderbolts." The cover on the right is cartoonist Art Castillo's proposed changes for a 3¢ stamp commemorating the Palomar telescope, "a six to seven-million-dollar hoax."

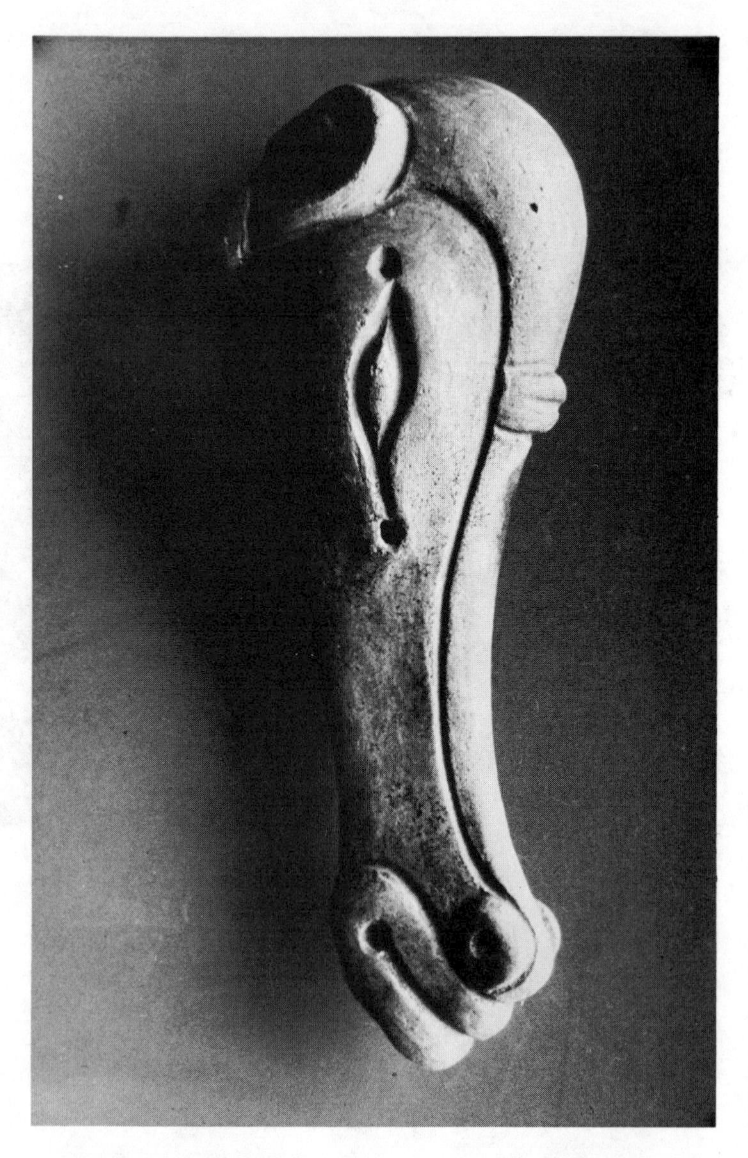

15. Less than two years ago *The New York Times* identified this stone carving as a "horse-like figure found among ancient Arawak remains near Orinoco River, Venezuela." Since horses had not yet arrived in the Americas when the figure was carved, the conclusion was that it represents a sea horse. Credit: *The New York Times.*

Chapter Seven

Down the Rabbit Hole

> As for the idea that sun-spots may exert specific influence on the weather of different parts of the Earth, it is beneath the dignity of science to discuss a notion worthy only of the first beginnings of astrology.
>
> Proctor, *Old and New Astronomy*

One thing led to another. When I began my study of Fort, the first thing was obviously to read every word of the omnibus edition of his work, *The Books of Charles Fort,* and make notes. Then it occurred to me that I could not make sense of Fort's data, scattered as they are through the 1,062 pages of the omnibus, unless I typed them on file cards and arranged them by date. When I finished I had twelve hundred file cards. From this it was only a step to making tables of the data, broken down into categories, and then it was too late

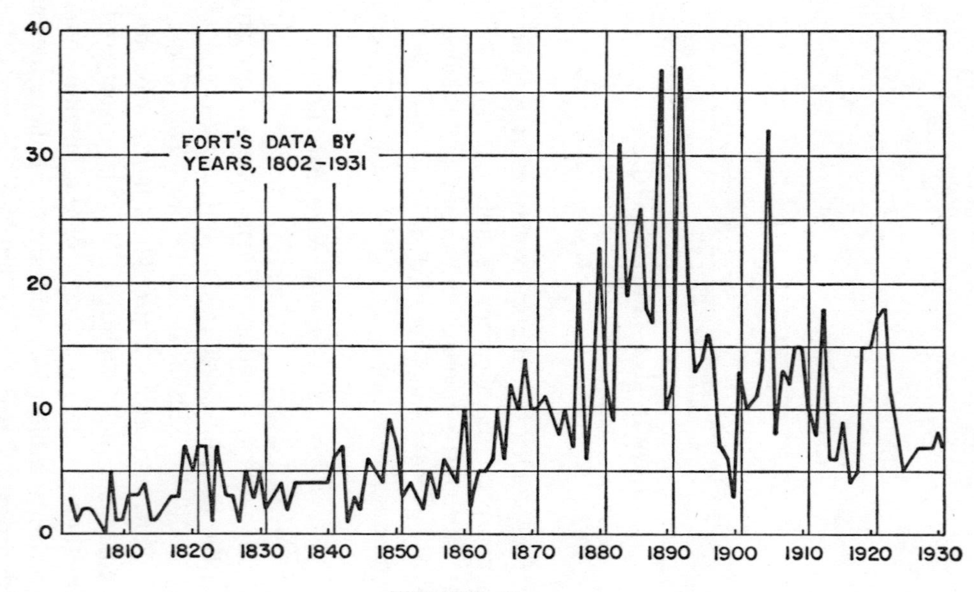
FORT'S DATA BY YEARS, 1802-1931
NUMBER OF REPORTS
0
10
20
30
40
1810
1820
1830
1840
1850
1860
1870
1880
1890
1900
1910
1920
1930

FIGURE 2

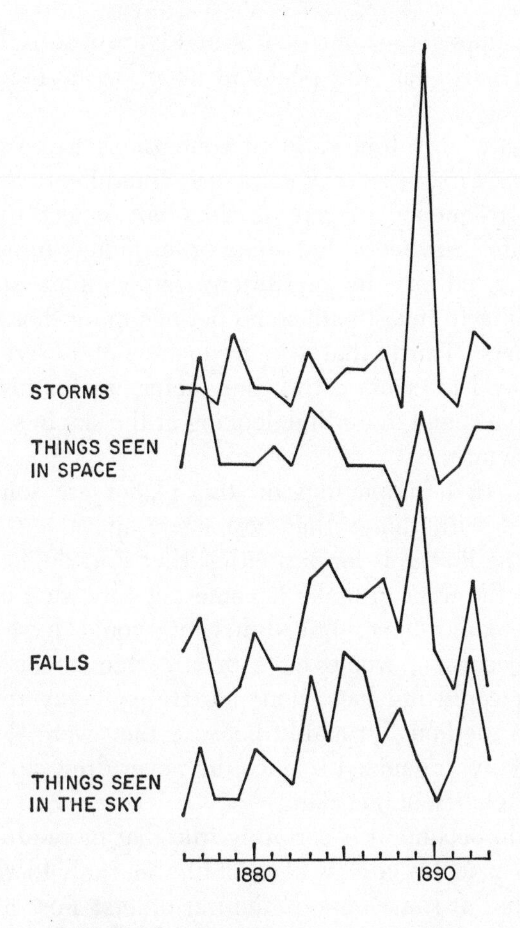

FIGURE 3

to draw back–I had to make charts. I made a chart of all the data by years (Figure 2). I made charts of storms, charts of falls, of things seen in space and things seen in the sky (Figure 3).

When I compared these charts, something interesting began to emerge. During the period 1877–1892, the correlations among the four charts in Figure 3 are obvious —note in particular the peaks at 1877, 1883, 1889, and 1892.

There are only four rational conclusions to be drawn from this. First, that the data are fraudulent. Second, that the frequency of reports does not reflect the frequency of occurrences, but some other factor—interest of newspaper editors in mysterious happenings, say, or Fort's whim to investigate some periods more thoroughly than others. Third, that the frequency of *observations* is influenced by some extraneous factor, as, for instance, that people spend more time looking at the sky in summer than in winter.

Fourth, that happenings on this planet are somehow connected with things that happen in space.

As to the first, this implies either that Fort deliberately "cooked" the data to make it come out this way, or that I did. I could have, but didn't; it would have been foolish, because I would have been certain to be found out. Fort could not have done so. He explicitly rejected statistical methods, probably because they were the tool of his enemy, organized science; he never drew up tables or made charts of his data.

As to the second, it is certainly true that more attention has been paid by editors of scientific journals to reports of this kind at some periods than at others: Fort himself remarks on the increasing orthodoxy of British scientific periodicals after about 1860. There is no evidence, however, that this interest fluctuated so steeply from one year to the next. During the period we are concerned with, 1877 to 1892, it remained high. The words "newspaper editors," above, are a red herring. Fort drew most of his data from scientific publications, not newspapers. Nor is it possible to imagine that he thoroughly investigated the year 1877 and then relaxed his interest when he came across the date 1878. His own account of his methods makes it clear how meticulously he covered the whole ground, not once but again and again.

As to the third, we are dealing with annual data. If there are seasonal variations, they must cancel out.

Even among ordinary natural phenomena, not all variations are annual or seasonal. Lynx abundance in Canada has been found to vary in a regular cyclical pattern with a period of about 9.6 years. Snowshoe rabbit abundance in Canada has been found to have the same cyclical pattern, and the same turning points: that is, when rabbits are abundant, lynx are abundant.

The connection between these two patterns is easy to see—the lynx prey on the rabbits. But the same cyclical pattern, and the same turning points, have been found in more than twenty other phenomena. (See Figure 4.) Other cycles have been found which behave in the same way. It is not easy to find a causal connection between marriages in St. Louis, Nile floods, immigration, and Java tree rings; yet all these show the same periodicity (approximately 18.2 years) and the same turning points.

This brings us back to a neglected question about the lynxes and the rabbits. We can say, roughly speaking, that the rabbit cycle is the cause of the lynx cycle. But what is the cause of the rabbit cycle?

The length of the cycle, 9.6 years, does not correspond to any seasonal variation. If one peak falls in mid-January, 1940, for example, the next will be in September, 1949; the next in March, 1959. Why should rabbit populations vary in this offbeat way, like an unregulated clock?

The conclusion is inescapable that these cycles of activity, which pass through our world like radio waves

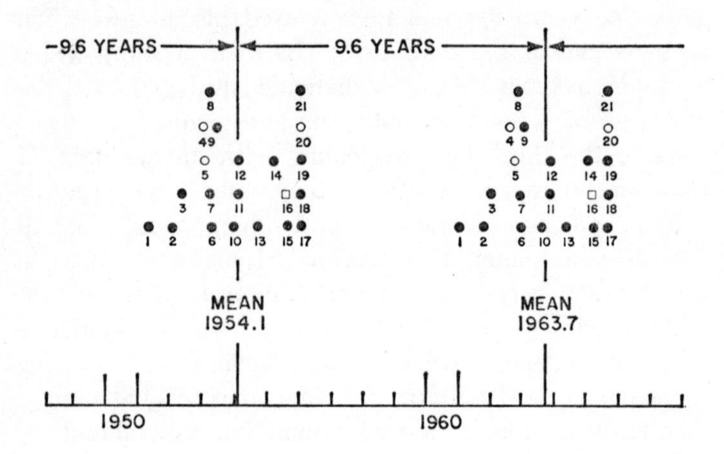

FIGURE 4

The Timing of the Ideal Turning Points of 21 Different Phenomena Alleged to Fluctuate in 9.6-Year to 9⅔-Year Cycles.

Solid dots indicate crests; open dots indicate troughs; the open square indicates the average of the turning points of 45 average 9.6-year cycles in precipitation.

1. Barometric Pressure, Paris
2. Rabbit (Snowshoe) Abundance, Canada
3. Tree-Ring Widths, Arizona
4. U-Magnetic Value
5. Wheat Acreage Harvested, U.S.A.
6. Wheat Prices, Europe
7. Chinch Bug Abundance, Illinois
8. Salmon Abundance, Canada
9. War (International Battles)
10. Lynx Abundance, Canada
11. Salmon Abundance, England
12. Tent Caterpillar Abundance, New Jersey
13. Ozone Content of Atmosphere, London and Paris
14. Heart Disease, New England

of enormous length, must have a common cause. The cause of the cycles, the controlling force that keeps them in synchrony, must lie outside the Earth.

Everyone is familiar with the influence of solar and lunar cycles on our planet—sunrise and sunset, winter and summer, the tides. Many people are aware that sunspot cycles and solar flares have an influence on our weather; some may have heard of the recent studies which show a definite lunar influence on rainfall. Few realize that recent investigations have confirmed an old and unfashionable belief: that the *planets* of the solar system also affect our lives.

John H. Nelson, Propagation Analyst for RCA Communications, Inc., has for years been making long-range forecasts of magnetic storms based on configurations of the planets. Specifically, he has found that when one or more of the other planets are in conjunction, opposition or quadrature with the Earth, he can expect a magnetic storm. Since these storms disrupt radio communications, it is important for RCA to have accurate forecasts. Nelson's accuracy, using these methods, is better than 90 percent.

The sensitivity of living organisms to variations in terrestrial magnetism, electrical potential, solar emissions, and cosmic rays has been established by the research

---

15. Rainfall, London
16. Precipitation, 45 Stations, Worldwide
17. Coyote Abundance, Canada
18. Marten Abundance, Canada
19. Mink Abundance, Canada
20. Muskrat Abundance, Canada
21. Run-off, Rihand River, India

Adapted from *Cycles,* July 1967

of Frank A. Brown, Morrison Professor of Biology at Northwestern University. In a series of famous experiments, Brown has shown that living creatures have "biological clocks" which keep perfect local time, even when they are in dark chambers under constant air pressure, humidity, and temperature. Oysters, for example, transported from Long Island Sound to Brown's laboratories in Evanston, Illinois, at first opened and closed their shells in the same rhythm as before. After about fifteen days, however, they had adjusted their rhythm so that their shells opened, not when it was high tide in Long Island Sound, but when it *would have been* high tide in Evanston, if Evanston were on the ocean—that is, when the moon passed the local meridian.

Georgio Piccardi, Director of the Institute for Physical Chemistry in Florence, has been measuring the speed of chemical reactions daily since 1951. It has long been known that the speed with which many reactions take place varies unaccountably; Piccardi has now shown that this speed is determined by solar activity as well as by the lunar cycle.

Even more astounding is the research of Michel Gauquelin of the Psychophysiological Laboratory at Strasbourg University. Gauquelin, in the course of a statistical study designed to test the claims of astrology, came across one set of results which surprised him and which he accepted with reluctance. "In one of our research samples—composed of the birth dates of 576 members of the French Academy of Medicine—the frequency of the position of certain planets was altogether unusual. The phenomenon did not correspond to any of the traditional laws of astrology, but it was interesting, nevertheless. What we had observed was that a large number of future great physicians were born when the planets

Mars and Saturn had just risen or culminated in the sky."[119]

A second study, of 508 other eminent physicians, produced the same result. Gauquelin then embarked on a third study of major proportions. He tabulated the dates and times of birth of every famous Frenchman he was able to find. He went to other countries to consult libraries and civic records: Italy in 1956, Germany in 1957, Belgium and Holland in 1958. In this way he collected nearly 36,000 birthdates.

The statistical pattern persisted. Gauquelin discovered that scientists, physicians, athletes, military men, and businessmen tend to be born when Mars has just risen or culminated (reached the zenith); Jupiter shows a similar correlation with military men, politicians, actors, journalists, and playwrights; Saturn with scientists and physicians; and the Moon with politicians and writers. These records had to be gathered with great care, since he needed to know not merely the date and place, but the hour and minute of birth; also whether or not birth had been hastened surgically or by the use of drugs. (In these cases, the data showed no correlation with planetary positions.)

Gauquelin rejected the idea that the planets exert some occult influence over the child at the moment of birth, determining his future career; instead, he proposed a hereditary predisposition, in persons of certain genetic patterns, to be born at the rise or culmination of certain planets.

To test this hypothesis, he worked for over five years on birth records of several counties in the Paris region, and collected data on more than thirty thousand parents and their children. Statistical analysis showed that the probability of a child's being born at the rise or culmination of a given planet was higher if one of his parents had been born when the same planet was at the same position in the sky; it was higher still if both parents had been born at a similar time. The correlation was so high that the probability of this result occurring by chance was only 1 in 500,000.

I went on making charts. I made charts of monthly data, and at one point I had a monster—a strip of chart paper thirteen feet long, with a dot of color for each datum, a different color for each category—and no idea what to do with it. I sought help from those who knew more about charts than I did, and had some interesting correspondence. I mentioned my monthly data once or twice, and was told to forget it. I went back to my monthly data.

C. L. Mallows of Bell Telephone Laboratories, who kindly put the annual Fort data through a computer analysis, pointed out that the chart is divided into three unequal sections; the first and third are irregular and show little evidence of other than random variability. The middle section, however, is characterized by "large swings and a very strong three-year periodicity." He suggested that these three sections should be analyzed separately, since averaging them in together would tend to blur the results.

I had already drawn a twelve-month table of this middle section, and I thought I saw in it a tantalizing hint that these periodicities had something to do with the oppositions of Mars. With the aid of an ephemeris, I worked out dates for the oppositions, conjunctions, and quadratures of Mars. When I laid them out on my table of data, I saw that the lines they formed passed through all the heaviest clusters, and that nearly every monthly count that rose above three lay within a month on one side or the other of an opposition, conjunction, or quadrature of Mars. (A planet is said to be in opposition with the Earth when the Sun and the planet are on opposite sides of the Earth; it is in conjunction when the Sun and the planet are on the same side of the Earth, and in quadrature when the Sun, the Earth, and the other planet form a right angle. Oppositions, conjunctions and quadratures are called "epochs" by astronomers.) Wishing to be fair, I worked out dates for the other planets as well, but found no correlations above the chance level for any except the inferior conjunctions of Venus. (Inferior conjunctions are those in which the other planet is on the near side of the sun; when it's on the far side, that's a superior conjunction.)

I made two more charts, assigning arbitrary values of 3 to Mars and 2 to Venus, since the data seemed to show that the influence of Venus was less pronounced. These charts took the form of a series of peaks and valleys; in the case of Mars, from 0 (no influence) to 3 (maximum influence) and back to 0. Combining these two charts gave me an irregular jagged line, which I superimposed on the chart of Fort's monthly data. The positive correlation between these two lines is such that the probability it could be due to chance is less than 1 percent. Chance, in other words, would not be expected to bring about this result more often than once in a hundred times—meaning, in this case, once in sixteen hundred years. (See Figure 5.)

This is what we come down to, and what I ask you to face: this correlation establishes a strong presumption that the phenomena we are talking about are *real.* Even if we dismiss all these reports as hallucinations, misinterpretations, and fabrications, the correlation remains

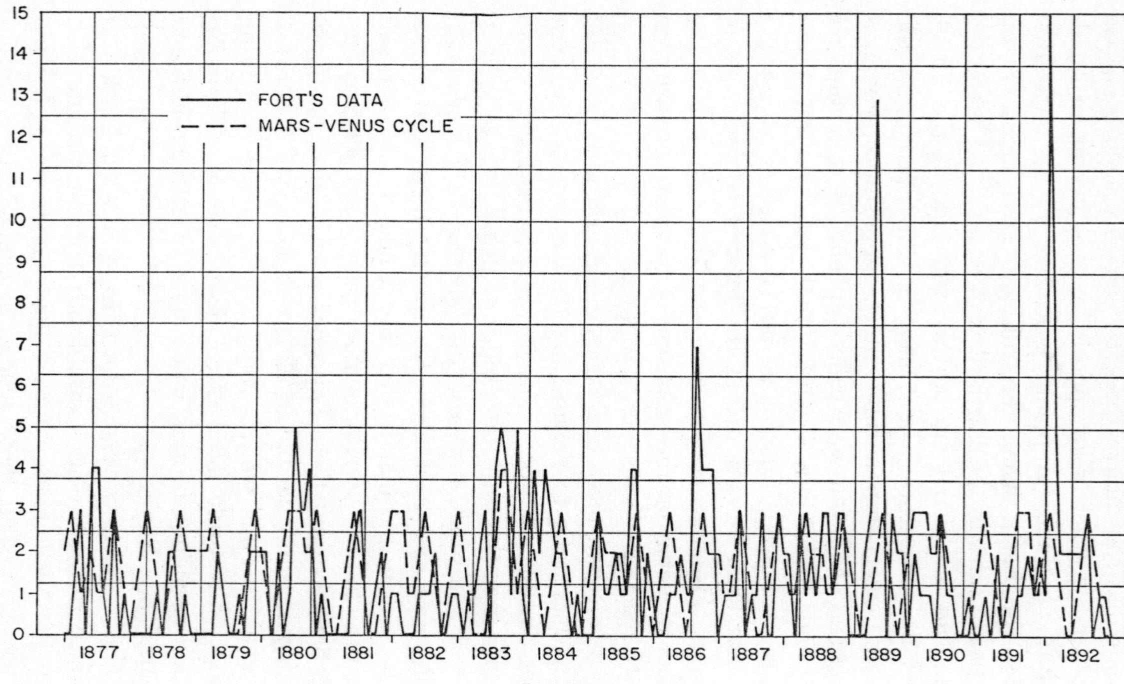

FORT'S DATA
MARS-VENUS CYCLE
15
14
13
12
11
10
9
8
7
6
5
4
3
2
1
0
1877
1878
1879
1880
1881
1882
1883
1884
1885
1886
1887
1888
1889
1890
1891
1892

FIGURE 5

and we have still to account for it. We can do so only by assuming that *the disposition of human beings to hallucinate, misinterpret, and fabricate such phenomena* is itself influenced by planetary movements.

Let us now imagine, for the sake of argument, that under certain conditions of gravitic and electromagnetic strain in the solar system, channels open through which material objects can reach the Earth from parts unknown, or can be transferred from one part of the Earth's surface to another. If these channels are electromagnetic in nature, we may approach an answer to the puzzling question of selectivity: why do frogs fall, and only frogs; or only insects, or only stones? All living things have electric charges, and it is possible to imagine that an electromagnetic field would discriminate between them.

When the things that fall are of familiar kinds, the overwhelming probability is that they come from somewhere else on the Earth's surface. (It is not theoretically impossible that identical species should have developed on another planet, but it is so unlikely that we may as well forget it.) It is a striking fact, however, that although frogs, fish, and so on have often been seen falling, they have never been seen *rising*. Do whirlwinds pick up little frogs from A and drop them at B? Fort thought this sometimes happened; but he balked at believing in a whirlwind that would deposit all its frogs in one place, and all its fish, mud, and miscellaneous debris somewhere else.

Fort gives us a few instances of alleged ascents: two of washing from a line, one of sheets of paper, one of miscellaneous trash from a courtyard, two of stones from a field, and one other which we may tentatively class with these: in the case of one of the falls of leaves, it is said that two children were drawn toward the center of the disturbance, and that their parents held them back. Of a similar kind are the stories of the old couple in the hotel room, who were convinced that the floor had opened under them, and of the college students who fought to keep one of their number from being snatched away by something invisible.

But the records of falls outnumber these by a factor of several hundred. We are therefore forced to consider that a simple "up in one place, down in another" explanation will not fit. If we are unwilling to believe that there are frogs on Venus, or "vermin" in comets, as Velikovsky intimates, we are left with two other possible explanations. First, we might suppose, rather fancifully, that when objects move along these channels, they move not only in space but in time. That would help to explain why persons who vanish are never seen again, and why no antecedents can be found for some persons who appear. We might argue further that these transfers need not be evenly distributed in time, and that we simply happen to be on the receiving end of them.

The other possibility is that, as some writers have suggested, there are other Earths all around us, each separated from the others and from us along a fourth spatial dimension: and that the gravitic and electromagnetic strains we have already mentioned cause points of contact to open between one or more of these and our own Earth. If such transfers take place, they would neatly explain everything that is otherwise inexplicable about these falls and appearances. If rain falls on one tree in Georgia, it is falling through such a channel from another Earth; if rain falls from our sky, through such a channel, to another Earth, the fact will never be noticed.

Corroboration for this notion turned up unexpectedly

when I talked to George R. Lewis of the Department of Computer Science at Clarion State College in Clarion, Pennsylvania. Dr. Lewis has discovered that when a radiation source and parabolic reflectors are placed in a certain geometrical relationship, the output of energy is greater than the input, by a factor which varies unpredictably. When asked about the source of the additional energy, he says forthrightly, "I know where it comes from—the fourth dimension!" The effect occurs with any kind of radiation, from radio to light-waves. If it could be brought under control, it could be used to generate free power and light; it could be a military weapon, more destructive than a fission bomb; on a micro-scale, it could be used to kill cancer cells.

I asked Lewis, "What if you used light, and put a series of lenses at the focus of the beam? Would there be an image, and if so what would you see?" He nodded, and his eyes twinkled: he had already thought of that. What *would* he see—another Earth, and another Professor Lewis, looking back?

Let us suppose that a channel opens between this Earth and another, where the surface is a few hundred feet, or a few thousand feet higher. Then things fall, from that Earth to this. Frogs, minding their own affairs in a pond, feel the bottom drop out. Next moment they are flopping and bouncing in a city street. Ice, floating in a stream, falls. Stones from a bank fall; dusts from a desert, muds from a river bottom.

Eppur se muove.

If there are local anomalies or discontinuities in the space-time frame, they may be more common than we have so far imagined. We have been discussing things that fall from the sky, or from "appearing points" below the ceilings of houses; but these discontinuities may occur also at the level of the Earth's surface, or below it. All over the world, objects have been found in unaccountable locations: stone wedges in trees, Roman coins in Indian burial mounds in North America; nails in blocks of stone.

One of the most striking examples is that of the Chinese seals found over a wide area in Ireland. These are not the kind of seals with fur and flippers, but cubes of jade, each with a carved animal seated on it, inscribed with ancient Chinese characters. In 1852 about sixty had been found, scattered as if at random in field and forest.

But while we are speaking of the other sort of seals, there was the one that appeared in 1926 in a pond in Hampstead Heath, London. Three months later, in the same pond, another seal appeared. Or consider the curious appearances and disappearances of the Barbary apes: "The numbers sometimes change in the most unaccountable way. Well-known monkeys are absent for months, and then reappear with new, strange adult monkeys of a similar breed. Those who know Gibraltar will agree that there is not a square yard on the Rock where they could have hidden."[120]

In April, 1967, oil from a grounded tanker was all over Normandy beaches. A few weeks later, there was oil on New England beaches; but this time, no grounded tanker.

Other things occasionally turn up where we know they ought not to be. Then scientists explain. It is known that a species of European snail-like marine organisms somehow reached eastern North America in prehistoric times: the puzzle is how they did it. The New York *Times*, February 5, 1968, quoting Dr. Junius B. Bird of the American Museum of Natural History, suggests that they crossed the Atlantic by hitchhiking on driftwood. And in the *Times*, April 11, 1968, there's a lovely thing: a photograph of a prehistoric horse-head figure found in Venezuela. The caption reads: "Horse-like figure found among ancient Arawak remains near Orinoco River, Venezuela. Horses were unknown in the Americas then, and it may represent a sea horse."

Human beings, too, have appeared and vanished. The most famous disappearance was that of Benjamin Bathurst, a special envoy of the British government, who on November 25, 1809, stopped at the little village of Perleberg, Germany, to change horses. In the presence of his valet and his secretary, he walked around the horses, and was never seen again.

Fort gives numerous instances of people found wandering, often naked, and unable to give any account of themselves. Some did not speak any known language. Kaspar Hauser, who appeared in Nuremberg in May, 1828, is the best known of these cases, but there are many others. Fort suggests that Cagliostro may have been one. ("Hosts of persons suppose that the exposure of Cagliostro, as an imposter, is as firmly, or rationally, established, as are the principles of geology, or astronomy. And it is my expression that they are right about this.")[121]

There are two suggestive items in Fort about persons who both disappeared and appeared. One is that of a young man named Leonard Wadham, who was found in a state of agitation near Dunstable, thirty miles from London, and who said that he had been walking on a street in South London; how he had got to Dunstable, he did not know. Then there is the case of Mrs. Alice Hilton, of Wigan, England, who was found unconscious on the shore of the Isle of Man, near Douglas, and who died without regaining consciousness. It was supposed that she had arrived on the boat from England on February 3,

1905; she had last been seen in Wigan on February 2, on her way to Ince to visit a cousin.

At intervals of three to five years, lemmings swarm down from the highlands of Norway and Sweden toward the sea. Other periodic outbreaks of rodents are known, as well as occasional outbreaks such as the wave of mice that overwhelmed Kern County, California, in January, 1927; but the lemmings are unique in that when they have crossed the lowlands, eating everything in their path, they swim out into the ocean and are drowned.

The interesting question here is: where does the next wave of lemmings come from? It has been suggested that "the survivors make their way back to the highlands, where they remain until their numbers increase again." I have been unable to find any testimony of a witness who has seen these survivors. Every account of lemming migrations emphasizes the irresistible force of the migratory urge. "The lemmings advance steadily and slowly, regardless of all obstacles, swimming streams and even lakes of several miles in breadth and committing considerable devastation on their line of march by the quantity of food they consume. In their turn they are pursued and harassed by crowds of beasts and birds of prey, as well as by man, and even domestic animals such as cattle, goats and reindeer join in the destruction, stamping them to the ground with their feet and even eating their bodies. Numbers also die from an epidemic disease known as 'lemming fever' (apparently tularemia), seemingly epidemic from overcrowding. None returns and the onward march of the survivors never ceases until they reach the sea, into which they plunge and are drowned."[122]

In order to account for the continued survival of the lemmings, we must suppose either that some lemmings turn back at the last moment, an event which has never been observed, or that some lemmings in the highlands do not take part in the mass migration at all. If the latter is the case, we would suppose that the migratory instinct would have been bred out of the race long ago, since only those who lacked it would survive to breed.

In this connection, it is interesting to note that the history of the lemmings is "mixed with folk tales and improbable interpretations. We are told, for example, that in 1578 'in the entire surroundings of Bergen, there rained big yellow Mice which swam ashore when they fell into the water.' In September and October of the next year, Lemmings were also said to have fallen from the sky in the Bishopric of Bergen."[123]

In the year 1869, after a summer notable for its scarcity of insects, England was invaded by swarms of insects. Some of these were of familiar kinds, others were unknown. In July, drowned aphides turned the water into pea soup off the coast of Lincolnshire, and off the coast of Norfolk, there was "a band of drowned ladybirds, about ten feet wide, and two or three miles long." In August, more ladybirds, in such numbers that citizens had to band together to shovel them up and burn them. Then midges, winged ants, "thunder bugs," so-called by the inhabitants of Wingham and Adisham, who had never seen any such thing before; then beelike flies, in sky-darkening swarms; then thrips, "spinning jennys" that shrouded the buildings of Burntisland, Scotland, with their webs; then bees of an unknown species, clouded yellow butterflies, hummingbird hawkmoths, wasps, gnats, crane flies, white butterflies, beetles of a kind never seen before in Lincolnshire; then spiders and their webs raining from the sky "in wondrous quantities . . . covering fields, houses, and persons"; then locusts—a species never seen before in England or Europe.[124] It was a deluge of insects. Where did it come from? Many of these swarms were seen approaching the English coast from the Channel. Not one was seen anywhere in Europe.

In August, 1880, a cloud of long, black flies darkened the sky of Havre, France. This swarm had come from somewhere in the Channel. It had not been seen in England. Three days later, another cloud of long, black flies, at East Pictou, Nova Scotia. It took "twenty minutes in passing." On September 2, another swarm, off Norfolk, England. It overwhelmed a schooner for five hours. "The air became clear, about 4 P.M., when the flies were thrown overboard by shovelfuls, and the remainder were washed off the decks by buckets of water and brooms." On September 4, long black flies on the Hudson River, between New Hamburg and Newburgh. "It reached southward, from shore to shore, as far as the eye could see. The insects were flying northward, as thick as snow-flakes driven by a strong wind."[125] On the following day, another swarm came in from the ocean at Guysboro, Nova Scotia. These swarms were torpid, or exhausted; the insects fell into the water and died. Where had they come from?

Note that all these swarms appear to have arrived from the ocean. Those that inundated Great Britain could not have been British bugs blown out to sea and then back in again, as was suggested: all that summer of 1869, there had been such a dearth of insects in England that swallows had starved to death.

The disappearance of the crew and passengers of the *Mary* (not *Marie*) *Celeste* has been explained and explained, but never explained away. Fort gives many other examples of puzzling disappearances at sea. It may be said that, after all, no disappearance at sea is hard to explain. But what about the disappearance of airplanes, not over the sea or near it? On May 29, 1919, Captain Mansell R. James left Lee, Massachusetts, for Mitchel Field, Long Island. He was last seen over the Berkshires. No trace of his plane was ever found.

Or what about the curious case of the two British aviators who were sent on a routine reconnaissance over Mesopotamia in July, 1924? When the plane did not return, it was searched for and found, in the desert. Nothing was wrong with the plane, and there was gas in the tank. The two men, Flight-Lieutenant W. T. Day and Pilot Officer D. R. Stewart, were missing. In the sand their footprints could be seen. "They were traced, side by side, for some forty yards from the machine. Then, as suddenly as if they had come to the brink of a cliff, the marks ended."[126] The desert was searched, rewards were offered; but no further traces were found, and the mystery was never solved.

Is it thinkable that Captain James is still flying, in the air of some other Earth: or that Day and Stewart saw a mirage—a strange landscape where the desert of Mesopotamia ought to be—; that they landed, and walked into it?

We are trying to pull the threads together into a grand design. If there are tunnels in space-time, some may be near the surface of the Earth and people may blunder through them. Some may be high above the surface; and then we have rains of curious things. These holes in space may be of short or long duration; they may be recurrent: and then rains of blood, or stones, or frogs, fall again and again on the same small area of the Earth, because the place they are coming from is fixed with reference to the Earth, just as Fort said it was. And on occasion something may come through and stay awhile: something unknown, and vicious, or merely frightened. The unknown animals that have repeatedly ravaged flocks in England and elsewhere. The invisible beings that throw crockery, and break windows, and burn old ladies to death.

For some of the alternate Earths around us may be all but identical to ours, and some may be different in unpleasant ways.

Another heresy: when at last we land a manned space vessel on Mars, after all our pains to sterilize our probes and avoid contaminating other worlds with terrestrial organisms, will we find the Martian landscape covered with the dried traces of red rains, larvae, perhaps the desiccated bodies of little frogs?

If all this is true, and if we can find it out for certain, then we will see the gantries rust at Cape Kennedy, while men build other machines that probe for and find the invisible tunnels that lead to other worlds, not unthinkable light-years away, but as close as our own noses. And we will remember Fort's words:

"Nobody can give good attention to the data, if diverting his mind is consciousness, altogether respectful, of the scientists who say that there are no other physical worlds except planets, millions of miles away. . . ."

Chapter Eight

An Amazing Turn of Events

> Not so long ago science had to struggle to free itself from the shackles of religion. Now it is as dogmatic as religion once was. Ideas that were revolutionary, schismatic, and damned in the nineteenth century are beatified and pronounced infallible in the twentieth by the same guardians of dogma.
>
> Immanuel Velikovsky, "Answer to My Critics"

Why are these data damned? The usual syllogism goes: Science admits all factual evidence, and if necessary, revises its theories to fit. These data are excluded. Therefore they are not factual evidence.

If not, then what are they? They must be misinterpretations, hoaxes, and hallucinations. But thousands of people have witnessed falls of living things from the sky. When fish by the hundred fall into the streets of St.

Petersburg, Florida, and little boys are photographed seining them up from the gutters, is this a misinterpretation, a hoax, or a hallucination? By a misinterpretation, do we mean that they were not fish, or that instead of falling from the sky, they got into the streets in some other way (swimming up the storm sewers, for instance)? If it was a hoax, what ingenious fishmonger did it? Can hallucinations be photographed?

In fact, as Thomas S. Kuhn points out in his classic study, *The Structure of Scientific Revolutions,* it is a myth that science admits all factual evidence and revises its theories to fit. It is another myth that science grows in a linear and organic fashion, refining its theories step by step. Kuhn shows that any science, at a given time in history, is the prisoner of its basic preconceptions, which he calls "paradigms." Paradigms are defined as "universally recognized scientific achievements that for a time provide model problems and solutions to a community of practitioners."[127] Newtonian physics was such a paradigm; it was overthrown in the early years of this century—not by the graceful surrender of fair-minded scientists, as the Establishment now pretends, but only after a struggle that lasted twenty years. "Copernicanism made few converts for almost a century after Copernicus' death. Newton's work was not generally accepted, particularly on the Continent, for more than half a century after the *Principia* appeared. Priestley never accepted the oxygen theory, nor Lord Kelvin the electromagnetic theory, and so on."[128]

Galileo's discovery of the moons of Jupiter presents another example. Proctor gives this account of it in *Old and New Astronomy:*

> Naturally Galileo's discovery excited much interest among students of science, and much pain

> among those who, though calling themselves men of science, objected to see science pass beyond the limits with which they had been familiar. The weaker sort were offended for another reason, not being able to reconcile the discovery of a miniature of the solar system with the limited ideas they had formed about the universe. The aged mathematician Clavius expressed the opinion that the satellites of Jupiter were the children of Galileo's telescope; but the honest Jesuit frankly admitted his mistake when he had himself seen them. Deterred by this backsliding, those of feebler faith declined to look, lest they should be perverted by what they saw. Of one of these who died soon after, Galileo expressed the hope that the doubter might see the satellites on his way to heaven.
>
> When at length it was impossible to deny the existence of Jupiter's moons, it became the fashion to dispute the real character of their movements. It was argued that these objects do not revolve around the planet, but travel backwards and forwards behind its disc. Down to the middle of the seventeenth century many refused to believe that the satellites actually circulate around Jupiter.[129]

In a footnote Proctor added: "For aught I know the motion of the satellites may be denied to the present day. In the preface to the last edition (1823) of the *Principia,* edited by the learned Jesuits Le Sueur and Jacquier, there occurs the following remarkable passage: 'In adopting the theory of the Earth's motion, to explain Newton's propositions, we assume another character than our own, for we profess obedience to the decrees of the popes against the motion of the Earth.' It is, therefore, not wholly impossible that decrees may have been promulgated against the circulation of Jupiter's satellites also."

Kuhn shows that these recurrent crises are not only typical of science, but *necessary to its development*. The possession of a paradigm—an orthodox theory accepted by the whole community of scientists—alone makes it possible to define fruitful lines of investigation and concentrate on them. New data within a paradigm can only be accumulated, in many cases, by the use of highly sophisticated instruments which never would have been devised without the paradigm, and without long hours of laborious effort which, in the absence of the paradigm, never would have been invested.

Because the paradigm is essential, scientists tend to resist any data which will not fit into it. Nevertheless, anomalous observations accumulate over a period of decades until they can no longer be ignored: then that science is in a state of crisis, which is only resolved by the emergence of a new paradigm.

Scientists never willingly renounce the paradigm that has led them into crisis. "They do not, that is, treat anomalies as counterinstances, though in the vocabulary of philosophy of science that is what they are. . . . once it has attained the status of paradigm, a scientific theory is declared invalid *only if an alternate candidate is available to take its place.*"[130] (Italics mine.)

What a paradigm shift does is to break apart the whole field of a science and put the pieces together in a new way. This change cannot be accomplished without trauma, particularly in the case of older scientists who have devoted their whole lives to the paradigm under attack.

Aside from any personal interests involved, they may simply be incapable of the perceptual shift required.

Kuhn illustrates this by the 1949 experiments of J. S. Bruner and Leo Postman, in which subjects were shown anomalous playing cards (for instance, a red six of spades). When the exposures were brief, the subjects identified the cards without hesitation. Longer exposures produced hesitation and puzzlement; the subjects knew something was wrong, but could not tell what it was. The confusion increased with still longer exposures, until subjects suddenly crossed the threshold and identified the cards without difficulty. But some subjects never did adapt, and experienced "acute personal distress."

> In science, as in the playing card experiment, novelty emerges only with difficulty, manifested by resistance, against a background provided by expectation. *Initially, only the anticipated and usual are experienced even under circumstances where anomaly is later to be observed.*[131] (Italics mine.)

The inventors of new paradigms are men whose "attention has been intensely concentrated upon the crisis-provoking problems; usually, in addition, they are men so young or so new to the crisis-ridden field that practice has committed them less deeply than most of their contemporaries to the world view and rules determined by the old paradigm."[132] Dalton, for example, was not a chemist but a meteorologist; Newton was not a physicist but a philosopher and mathematician. Yet crossing-over of scientists from one field to another is fiercely resented by orthodox scholars. A recent example is that of James D. Watson and Francis Crick, who solved the structure of

DNA by invading a field which was not theirs, and who had to do much of their work by stealth because their superiors disapproved of it.[133]

The shift from one paradigm to another is a gradual process, which depends on the ability of the new paradigm to win disciples and converts. Once this shift has taken place, the former anomalies are seen as tautologies —statements of self-evident fact. Even the *data* have changed. Proust, for example, found an oxygen weight ratio for the two oxides of copper of 1.47–1 rather than the 2–1 ratio demanded by atomic theory. "Chemists could not, therefore, simply accept Dalton's theory on the evidence, for much of that was still negative. Instead, even after accepting the theory, they had still to beat nature into line, a process which, in the event, took almost another generation. When it was done, even the percentage composition of well-known compounds was different."[134]

Understanding this process makes it possible for us to realize that orthodox scientists *cannot accept anomalous data* and are frequently blind to it. It also helps us to understand how orthodox scientists, during the early period of a crisis, can respond to the presentation of anomalous data with arguments so clearly emotional and erroneous that they are otherwise difficult to explain.

One of the most instructive examples of this is the case of a scholar whose theories, at certain points, are strikingly similar to Fort's: Immanuel Velikovsky. In *Worlds in Collision,* and in two later books, *Ages in Chaos* and *Earth in Upheaval,* Velikovsky set forth his thesis that the Earth has repeatedly suffered near-collisions with other planets in historical times, most recently in the seventh century B.C., and that the records of the resulting global catastrophes are to be found in historical and archaeological documents, in folklore from many parts of the world, and in geological evidence.

The uproar over these books came as an unpleasant revelation to those of us who had thought of scientists as disinterested seekers of knowledge. A group of astronomers led by Harlow Shapley, then Director of Harvard College Observatory, mounted a campaign to prevent the publication of *Worlds in Collision;* failing that, to discredit it; finally, to force Macmillan to cease publication of the book by boycotting its textbook division.[135] Macmillan, which depended heavily on textbook sales, found so many heads of college departments refusing to see its salesmen that it was forced to give in. In June, 1950, although the book was already a best-seller, Macmillan turned it over to Doubleday (which has no textbook division). James Putnam, the Macmillan editor who signed the original contract for the book, was summarily dismissed from a post he had held for twenty-five years. Gordon Atwater, who had championed Velikovsky, was fired as Curator of Hayden Planetarium and Chairman of the Department of Astronomy of the American Museum of Natural History.

In their published attacks on Velikovsky, Harvard astronomers Cecelia Payne-Goposchkin and Donald Menzel consistently distorted what he had said, then mocked the distortions. It is difficult to see these misrepresentations as other than deliberate.

In "Worlds in Collision," a paper read on April 24, 1952, at the Symposium on Some Unorthodoxies of Modern Science, and published in the *Proceedings* of the American Philosophical Society, October, 1952, Mrs. Payne-Goposchkin tried to discredit Velikovsky's scholarship by saying that he had attributed statements to Herodotus and the Bible which are not to be found in these sources.

But in the passages in question, Velikovsky plainly indicated that in the first instance his sources were Apollodorus and Strabo (*Worlds in Collision,* p. 81), and in the second instance, the Talmud and Midrashim (*ibid.,* p. 231).

In "An Astronomer's Rejoinder," in *Harper's,*[136] Menzel described as Velikovsky's "basic hypothesis" the idea that "the solar system is really a giant atom." In his "Comment on Dr. Menzel's Rejoinder," Eric Larrabee noted: "The atomic model is not Velikovsky's 'basic hypothesis.' It is mentioned only once in *Worlds in Collision* (pp. 387–88) and then only in a context indicating the author's awareness that it is no longer current and that many dissimilarities exist between the atom and the solar system."

Speaking of Velikovsky's theory that Venus was expelled from Jupiter as a comet and in close passages with Earth and Mars altered their orbital and rotational periods by electric discharges, Menzel said: "Electromagnetic forces—never exactly specified—were supposedly responsible for Venus's running amuck." In the next paragraph he added: "There is not a single equation to show how these electromagnetic fields could influence the motion of one planet and not of the others." But Velikovsky never suggested that electromagnetic forces were responsible for the expulsion of Venus from Jupiter.

As for Velikovsky's successful prediction of radio emissions from Jupiter, Menzel said: "Since the idea is wrong, any seeming verification of Velikovsky's prediction is pure chance." Larrabee commented: "Students of scientific method will be interested in this remarkable sentence."

One of the most incredible performances was that of Lloyd Motz, an astronomer at Columbia University, who was one of two signers of a letter to *Science*[137] (the other was Princeton physicist V. Bargmann), pointing out that three of Velikovsky's predictions had been verified and urging that his theories be given objective consideration. The writers emphasized that they did not believe Velikovsky was correct; they merely believed he should get a fair hearing.

In the April, 1967, issue of *Yale Scientific* magazine, an issue devoted to Velikovsky, Motz undertook to explain his objections to Velikovsky's theories. In his article, "Velikovsky—a Rebuttal," he began by discussing Velikovsky's "assumption that Venus erupted from Jupiter in a kind of volcanic process," and in the course of rebutting this assertion—which Velikovsky never made—he himself made a series of elementary scientific and mathematical errors. In his response in the same issue, "A Rejoinder to Motz," Velikovsky calmly pointed these out one by one, and left Motz's argument in ribbons.

Motz made the following statements:

The sun's "distance from Jupiter is about 5 times that of the earth from Jupiter." (He should have said "of the sun from the earth." In effect, Motz had the ratio backwards, and this made nonsense of all his following calculations.)

Jupiter's escape velocity "is about six times the speed of escape from the earth or about 70 km per sec (7,000,000 cm per sec)." (The correct value is 59 km/sec. Furthermore, as Velikovsky pointed out, Motz had neglected to subtract from this figure the rotational velocity of Jupiter at the equator, which is about 13 km/sec. "In squaring 70 (7,000,000 cm per sec) instead of 46 (4,600,000 cm per sec), he multiplied (squared) the error, and all figures that follow are correspondingly wrong." Nor is this all; Velikovsky went on to point out that 100 percent of escape velocity is needed only for an orbit extending to infinity; for an elliptical orbit, only about 71 percent of this velocity is needed. Finally, he noted that "the conservation of angular momentum requires that Jupiter slowed in its rotation upon ejecting Venus; therefore, even with the above corrected figures, it would be improper to calculate the conditions for escape on the basis of the present (resultant) angular momentum or speed of rotation of Jupiter.")

"The Roche limit for Jupiter, which is the region extending outward from its surface in which, through its tidal action, it can break a body into pieces, is of the order of one million miles." (The correct value is about 100,000 miles. Velikovsky notes that if the Roche limit were where Motz says it is, four of Jupiter's satellites would be inside it.)

I think Velikovsky's opponents were betrayed into these gross and obvious errors by their lack of practice in debating scientific subjects with outsiders. If they had been dealing with another member of the guild, they would have been much less likely to appeal to authority, to make careless errors of fact and indefensible dogmatic statements, partly because they would know other scientists would pounce on these immediately, and partly because there is a standard of decorum in scientific debate. But it is axiomatic that when you are debating professional matters with an amateur, these standards do not apply: what you want to do then is to shut him up by the quickest and most effective means. Among these means are dogmatic statements and appeals to authority. Since the object was to silence Velikovsky, not to examine his position, it did not seem to matter much whether the arguments used were correct or not, since it was known that Velikovsky was wrong—if not for these reasons, then for other reasons.

The same assumption also led Velikovsky's attackers,

by a familiar psychological process, to assume that since Velikovsky was wrong, *evidence to that effect must exist.* Thus more than one of Velikovsky's opponents began by remarking confidently that his assertions about the solar system could not be correct, since existing astronomical records show perfect regularity as far back as the third millennium B.C. But this does not happen to be true.

In "Disciplines in Collision," in *Harper's,*[138] the astrophysicist John Q. Stewart asserted that the global cataclysms described by Velikovsky could not have occurred in the period between 1500 and 700 B.C., because "Egyptian obelisks and columns still stand at Thebes which were standing then, though even moderate jerking of the ground would upset them on their narrow bases," and because the Pyramids show no signs of wrenching by earthquakes. But neither of these things happens to be true, either.

The scientists were betrayed by their own sense of professional superiority, and by their perfect confidence that Velikovsky's gun was not loaded.

It is instructive to read Stewart's article in *Harper's* together with Velikovsky's reply which follows it in the same issue. Velikovsky's replies to his critics, on those occasions when he has been allowed to reply, have been models of scientific decorum; they are factual, objective, and dignified.

The world has already been turned topsy-turvy, not by Velikovsky but by his opponents, when the "charlatan" defends himself objectively and with restraint, while the leaders of the scientific establishment behave like ruffians.

But what is the cause of all this fury? To explain it, we must go back a long way.

In the nineteenth century the warfare between science and religion became a war between gradualism and catastrophism. The Velikovsky affair is only the latest skirmish in this war, which originally had religious motivations on both sides. The earliest geologists and paleologists held the view that the Earth had undergone a series of violent catastrophes, each followed by a new creation. In this way they explained the geological record and the fossil evidence of the sudden appearance of new species. To the rationalists who followed them, however, special creation was unacceptable and *therefore* catastrophism had to be rejected too. In its place they put gradualism, the dogma of continuous slow evolution and of gradual changes in the Earth's surface: they maintained that the Earth had undergone only gentle changes of the kind that can still be observed: weathering, the slow uplifting and slow subsidence of portions of the Earth's crust, and so on. This view became dominant in the later nineteenth century and is now so familiar that its origins have been lost to view. But old fears die hard, and to this day many scientists feel that any discussion of catastrophism is dangerous because it may bring back special creation with it.

All these theological and antitheological considerations have nothing to do with the question of whether, in fact, the Earth has suffered catastrophic changes in the past. The evidence that it has is extensive. The gradualists have never denied that this evidence exists, but have explained it away, saying for example that the sudden appearance and disappearance of species is due to gaps in the paleontological record, or to slow changes in climate; and that the bones of extinct mammals, found broken and packed together by hundreds in such places as La Brea Tar Pits in California, are those of animals which came to drink in a pool, became mired, and sank into quicksand.

In the eighteen years since the publication of *Worlds in Collision,* evidence confirming Velikovsky's theories has mounted. His suggestion that Jupiter emits radio noise was confirmed in 1955 by B. F. Burke and K. L. Franklin of the Carnegie Institution. Data collected by Mariner II in 1962 confirmed Velikovsky's statements about the extremely high temperature of Venus; radar observations in 1962 and 1966 revealed that the planet rotates retrogradely, with a period such that it turns the same face toward Earth at each passage—its rotation is "locked in" to the orbital revolution of Earth, strongly suggesting that the two planets must have had a close encounter in the past. Samples of rock taken from the Middle Atlantic Range startlingly confirm Velikovsky's hypothesis of repeated reversals of the Earth's magnetic polarity.

Physicists and astronomers since Newton have insisted that the motions of planetary bodies are governed by gravity and inertia, and by nothing else. In recent years it has become increasingly evident that this is not true. Electromagnetic interactions, whose nature and magnitude are still not well understood, must be taken into account. Interplanetary and even interstellar space is now seen, not as the sterile void of Newtonian physics, but as a rich stew of plasma, charged particles, radiation, and fields of force. The nature of gravitation itself is coming increasingly into question. The possibility is not to be excluded that a spectrum of gravitoelectric and gravitomagnetic forces, whose existence Einstein failed to prove, may nevertheless exist.

In an appendix to Mrs. Payne-Goposchkin's article, "Worlds in Collision," in the *Proceedings* of the American Philosophical Society,[139] Donald H. Menzel wrote: "If Velikovsky wants quantitative discussion, let us give him one. He expressed doubt about conventional celestial mechanics and he states a hypothesis on which to work: if the sun and planets carry electric charges of sufficient intensity, the electrical forces may overpower the gravitational. The laws of celestial mechanics are not in themselves sacred and, if Velikovsky wishes to question them, he is at liberty to do so." He went on to calculate that the charge on the sun necessary to produce an electrical attraction equal to one-tenth of its gravitational attraction to the Earth would be 10^{19} volts; and he said, "There is no possible mechanism by which the sun can hold such a charge."

Eight years later V. A. Bailey, Emeritus Professor of Physics at the University of Sydney, published a paper, in *Nature*,[140] maintaining that "the known orders of magnitude of five different astronomical phenomena" can be accounted for "by the single hypothesis that a star like the sun carries a net negative charge." He calculated this charge at 10^{19} volts.

> The idea that his "quantitative refutation of Velikovsky's wild hypothesis"—Menzel's own description of his contribution to the *Proceedings* in 1952—should now be brought to Velikovsky's support was intolerable to the Harvard astronomer. So, when he mailed his paper to *Harper's* in 1963, he also sent a copy to Bailey in Sydney and asked him in a covering letter to revoke his theory of electric charge on the sun. . . .
>
> Professor Bailey, taking exception to the idea that his own work should be abandoned to accommodate the anti-Velikovsky forces, prepared an article in rebuttal of Menzel's piece and submitted it to *Harper's* for publication in the same

> issue with Menzel's. Bailey had discovered a simple arithmetical error in Menzel's calculations, which invalidated his argument.
>
> The editors of *Harper's*, evidently taken aback by the heat of the controversy . . . rejected Bailey's offering, but agreed to print some of his comments if he would submit them in a brief letter. At the same time, however, Menzel was permitted to correct the arithmetical error pointed out by Bailey, and he did so without acknowledging the effect of the correction on his argument.[141]

In a curious way, Velikovsky seems to have been condemned, like Ralph Ginzburg (publisher of *Eros*), not for what he was selling but for the way it was promoted. Doubleday in its advertising called *Worlds in Collision* "the book about 'the day the sun stood still' and other Old Testament miracles, linking religious and scientific concepts of man's remote past," and ran a quotation from the Rev. Norman Vincent Peale: "These new theories are worthy of our consideration because they evidence the substantial basis of fact behind the Old Testament." This fundamentalist appeal may indeed have helped sales, but it is hard to understand how Velikovsky could be seriously charged with religious motivations by anyone who has read the book. There is not a word of theology in *Worlds in Collision;* Velikovsky does assert that certain Old Testament miracles really happened, including the parting of the Red Sea and the sun's standing still in Gibeon, but in each case he explains them as natural, not supernatural, events. Velikovsky, who after all is a Freudian analyst, even interprets the voice that spoke to Moses from

Sinai as the groaning of earth-strata in dislocation and the rumbling of volcanoes.

One of the most grotesque ironies in this whole situation is the fact that it was Newton, not Velikovsky, whose motivations were religious. Livio C. Stecchini writes, in *The Velikovsky Affair:*

> The concluding words of *Opticks* indicate that Newton, like others of his contemporaries, felt that, if the traditional views of cosmic order were abandoned, the foundations of morality would be undermined.[142]

He adds that Newton was "bent on proving that the machinery of the world is such a perfectly contrived system that it cannot be the result of 'mechanical cause,' but must be the result of an intelligent and consistent plan." The remainder of this passage is worth quoting at length.

> In order to support further the story of Genesis that the world was created by a single act, he argued also that the world is stable and has remained unchanged since creation. But he could not prove this point, since he admitted that, according to his theory, the gravitational pull among the several members of the solar system would tend to modify their orbits; hence, he begged the question and claimed that God in his providence must intervene from time to time to reset the clockwork of the heavens in its original state. This point of Newton's doctrine is well known, for it was the object of sarcastic comments by Newton's great rival in

> the mathematical field, Leibniz (1646–1716). As the latter observed, Newton cast God not only as a clockmaker, and a poor one at that, but also as a clock-repairman.[143]

The ten Biblical plagues of Egypt are explained by Velikovsky as consequences of the close passage of Venus and Earth: the plague of blood (red dust from the tail of the comet, turning the rivers red); the plagues of murrains and blains (irritations caused by the fall of dust); the plague of hail (Heb. *barad,* which Velikovsky points out is the word ordinarily used for "meteorites"); the destruction of the firstborn, which Velikovsky interprets as caused by an earthquake. Even the manna that nourished the Israelites in the wilderness is not excluded; according to Velikovsky, this substance was an edible carbohydrate which fell from the comet.

As for the second, third, fourth, and eighth plagues (frogs, lice, flies, and locusts), Velikovsky suggests that the heat generated by the comet passage may have caused frogs and insects to propagate at a feverish rate, or else that the tail of the comet Venus, and its parent body Jupiter, may have been full of "vermin." This is the weakest point of his argument, and he passes over it quickly. Falls of dust, ashes, and even edible organic substances may be ascribed to clouds of cosmic material, but any such explanation must also take into account the falls of living things; and it is difficult to imagine that organisms of known species exist on other planets of our solar system, or in outer space.

Yet throughout the historical period, black and red dusts and rains, stones, frogs, insects, and "manna" have gone right on falling from the sky.

Charles Fort lists seven falls of manna, of which the following is typical:

> In 1829 (Timb's *Year Book,* 1848-235) in Persia fell a substance that the people said they had never seen before. As to what it was, they had not a notion, but they saw that the sheep ate it. They ground it into flour and made bread, said to have been passable enough though insipid.[144]

If we accept both sets of data, the cataclysmic rains of Velikovsky and the gradualist rains of Fort, then either two processes are at work producing almost identical results, or the cataclysmic theory needs to be revised. It is not thinkable that clouds and gobbets of dust, stones, locusts, and flies, torn loose by planetary passages more than twenty-seven centuries ago, are still lurking in space, undispersed, for us to barge through on our trips around the sun.

For a clue to an alternative explanation, see this passage from Fort's *New Lands:*

> . . . we suppose the data are of physical relations between this earth and other worlds. We think of a difference of potential. There were tremendous detonations in the sky at the times of the falls of the little black stones of Birmingham and Wolverhampton, and the electric manifestations, according to descriptions in the newspapers, were extraordinary, and great volumes of water fell. Consequently the events were supposed to be thunderstorms. I suppose, myself,

> that they were electric storms that represented difference of potential between this earth and some region that was fixed, at least eleven years, over Birmingham and Wolverhampton. . . .[145]

Or this, two pages later:

> Latitudes and longitudes of bones, not in the sky, but upon the surface of this earth. Baron Toll and other explorers have, upon the surface of this earth, kicked their way through networks of ribs and protrusions of skulls and stacks of vertebrae, as numerous as if from dead land they had sprouted there. Anybody who has read of these tracts of bones upon the northern coast of Siberia, and of some of the outlying islands that are virtually composed of bones cemented with icy sand, will agree with me that there have been cataclysms of which conventionality and standardization tell us nothing. Once upon a time, some unknown force translated, from somewhere, a million animals to Colorado, where their remains now form great bone-quarries. Very largely do we express a reaction against dogmatism, and sometimes we are not dogmatic, ourselves. We don't know very positively whether at times the animal life of some other world has been swept away from that world, eventually pouring from the sky of Siberia and of Colorado, in some of the shockingest floods of mammoths from which spattered cats and rabbits, in cosmic scenery, or not. All that we can say is that when we turn to convention-

> ality it is to blankness or suppression. . . . Showers of frogs and showers of fishes that occur to this day—that they are the dwindled representatives to this day of the cataclysms of intenser times when the skies of this earth were darkened by afferent clouds of dinosaurs.[146]

If, in times of intensest strain, not merely particles but whole worlds break through into our solar system, then we can believe in catastrophic near-collisions, world-wrecking passages of planets, without the necessity of conceding that Venus was once a comet, or that it was expelled from Jupiter. We can imagine two solar systems, circling in disequilibrium, exchanging planets in a monstrous game of skittles, until everything that can break has been broken, and the captured moons peacefully circle their new primaries backwards; and the wreckage of a burst planet orbits between Mars and Jupiter. . . . And in our tidy Newtonian solar system, wound up once for all by the hand of the great clockmaker, the invisible worlds that did all the damage still pass like ghost ships; but now, instead of the groan of bedrock and the smashing of mountains, we get only some few thunderstorms and earthquakes, and a light sprinkle, now and then, of ash, or of blood, or of frogs.

In the first chapter of *Worlds in Collision,* Velikovsky draws our attention to the fact that if the Earth had been formed from a molten mass of intermingled elements, the oxygen in it would have been expected to combine with other elements: iron, for example; therefore the presence of iron in the Earth's crust, and free oxygen in the atmosphere, is unexplained. To account for these, we would have to imagine that the Earth was cold when it was formed, and later accumulated heat through radioactivity. But how could a cold Earth have been formed?

In chapter four of *Lo!,* Charles Fort wrote:

> It could be that, in reading what most persons think are foolish little yarns of falling stones, we are, visionarily, in the presence of cosmic constructiveness—or that once upon a time this whole earth was built up by streams of rocks, teleported from other parts of an existence. The crash of falling islands—the humps of piling continents—and then the cosmic humor of it all—or utmost spectacularity functioning, then declining, and surviving only as a vestige—or that the force that once heaped the peaks of the Rocky Mountains now slings pebbles at a couple of farmers, near Trenton, N.J.[147]

According to Velikovsky's timetable, the comet Venus, having been ejected from Jupiter as the result of a previous near-collision of Jupiter and Saturn, approached the Earth twice, with an interval of about fifty years, in the fifteenth century B.C. Its orbit perturbed by these passages, Venus then approached Mars repeatedly in the eighth century. In the final act Mars, similarly perturbed, approached the Earth.

The most serious difficulty in this theory is that of accounting for the present orbits of Earth and Venus. If any such near-collisions had occurred between Venus, Mars, and Earth, we would expect to find the orbits of all three planets highly eccentric. Mars, indeed, has an eccentric orbit; but the orbits of Earth and Venus are almost circular.

We can postulate electromagnetic forces acting between the Sun and the inner planets, which would have tended to reduce the eccentricity of their orbits; but in that case we have the very high eccentricity of the orbit of Mercury still to account for.

It should not be forgotten that no one has yet proposed a satisfactory theory to account for the observed motions of *any* planet in the solar system. We do not know how the planets and satellites were formed or how they took up their present orbits. We do not know why some of these orbits are nearly circular and some highly eccentric, why some are in the ecliptic plane and others not, why the motions of some are direct and some retrograde.

Triton, the largest satellite of Neptune, which must be a captured satellite because of its retrograde motion and high inclination, has a nearly circular orbit. Classical mechanics shows that this is impossible: nevertheless, there it is.

The whole dynamic pattern of the solar system is one of monstrous disarray. The orbit of Pluto is so eccentric that at perihelion it crosses the orbit of Neptune. Pluto's orbit is also highly inclined to the plane of the ecliptic—17.3 degrees. Few of the nine planets rotate upright in the planes of their orbits, as, according to classical mechanics, they ought to. The axial tilt of Uranus is 98 degrees—almost horizontal. The axial tilt of the Earth, which gives us our familiar seasons, is 23.5 degrees. This is within a few degrees of the axial tilts of Mars, Saturn, and Neptune. Why should these four planets be tilted to almost the same angle? For that matter, why should they be tilted at all?

The picture we get is either one of an orderly solar system which has been repeatedly and violently knocked out of alignment, or else that of a disorderly group of planets which has been partially coerced into order. In this perspective, the orbit of Venus is no more puzzling than any other. Venus *could not* have suffered a close encounter with the Earth and then assumed a nearly circular orbit. But the synchrony of its period of rotation with the Earth is hard to explain in any other way than by such an encounter.

Have it either way you like, the solar system is not the uniform and undisturbed clockwork mechanism Newton dreamed of. If classical mechanics cannot be reconciled with the motions we actually observe, then classical mechanics must be wrong.

Proctor says in *Old and New Astronomy,* "The great slope or tilt of the paths of the satellites [of Uranus] is even a more singular feature than the direction of their motion. Taken together with the undoubted retrograde motion of the satellite of Neptune, and the great inclination of the equator of Uranus, as indicated by the trend of the belts as well as by the measurements of the polar compression, we seem to have evidence that the two outer planets of the solar system, while moving in the same direction and approximately in the same plane as the inner planets, have been perturbed as to their axial motions. It seems difficult to believe that the comparative uniformity observable in the motions of the inner members of the group did not originally extend to the outer members; but there must either have originally been such a want of uniformity, or a change must have been brought about in the axial motions of Uranus and Neptune either by a sudden cataclysm, such as a blow from a comet, or by some slowly-acting force the existence of which we at present have no suspicion of."[148]

In *The New Intelligent Man's Guide to Science,* Isaac Asimov discusses the 1965 discovery by Thomas

Gold and others that Mercury does not keep one face eternally toward the sun, as we had thought, but rotates once in about sixty days. "If Mercury rotates as quickly as it does, Gold speculates, Mercury cannot have been in its present position for more than 400,000 years. This (if true) is an amazing turn of events."[149]

Chapter Nine

Stones, Blood, Fish

Resolute imagination is the beginning of all magical operations. Because men do not perfectly believe and imagine, the result is that arts are uncertain when they might be wholly certain.

Paracelsus (quoted in a letter from Aaron Sussman to Tiffany Thayer, March 8, 1935)

Let us now admit that many people will find in some of this data, and some people perhaps in all of it, a deeply and disturbingly irrational element. We may laugh now at those who once strenuously denied that stones fall from the sky, but they had a very good reason for it. Suppose you agree that an "impossible" thing has happened: what then? The fact cannot be fitted in anywhere, it is of no use, nothing can be done with it; it is like an extra piece in a jigsaw puzzle: if you once admit it, the puzzle can never be finished. The behavior of those who oppose the admission of certain facts may appear to be due to stupidity, or blind conservatism, or self-seeking, after the event, but at bottom I believe it is really due to this instinctive and perfectly reasonable dread of the piece that will not fit.

Therefore I consider that it is not enough to urge here that frogs really fall from the sky, that people are really incinerated by internal fires, that unknown bodies have been seen in space: we must also relate these facts in some rational way to the world we know: we must at least try to explain.

We come back again to the problem of selectivity. Why do frogs fall, and only frogs; or only fish, or lady-birds? If Chinese seals of jade fell on Ireland, from some Earth rotated with respect to ours so that our Ireland is their China—or from an Earth with a history different from ours, in which Ireland was colonized by the Chinese—still, why did jade seals fall, and only they? Why not chopsticks, buttons, combs, kettles, vases, pots and pans? Did some Chinese, born with a wild talent, dream avariciously of jade seals?

There is a strange irrational consistency in these phenomena. Think of the things that fall—stones, blood, fish, straw, ice, water. If a mind dreaming in symbols could make its symbols actual—or draw their counter-parts out of some other realm—these are some of the things we would expect. Then think of poltergeists, and of the strange animals that appear, attack herds and flocks and sometimes people, and then disappear. Who has not dreamed of invisible and malevolent beings, or of dimly seen four-footed killers in the twilight? If our minds indeed have the power to shape our reality, then we live in a universe of ultimate insecurity.

Charles L. Harness, a writer strongly influenced by Fort, suggests this in a brilliant story called "The New Reality."[150] In it he points out that the Babylonians, who were excellent mathematicians, thought the value of *pi* was 3, and draws the conclusion that in Babylonian times, the value of *pi was* 3. It follows that when men believed in a flat Earth, the Earth was flat; when they believed it was the center of the universe, it was. Whenever a few men committed themselves to new beliefs, and convinced others, then reality changed.

Any such system would tend to be self-perpetuating and unbreakable, because observation would inevitably support whatever theory was universally believed in; but fortunately for us, there have always been dissenters, cranks, and madmen.

We dream of catastrophes, earthquakes, volcanic eruptions, floods, fires. Earthquakes, volcanic eruptions, floods, and fires occur in patterns whose causes are unknown. Airplane crashes, gas explosions, even bus accidents, come in waves. We dread these things and they happen. Do they happen because we dread them?

In 1915 Percival Lowell predicted an unknown trans-Neptunian planet on the basis of his analysis of perturbations of Uranus. In 1930 Clyde Tombaugh discovered the planet Pluto, "less than six degrees from one of the two alternate positions predicted 15 years before." But the mass of Pluto turned out to be less than one sixty-sixth of the mass Lowell had assumed in his calculations. Therefore the success of the prediction was "purely accidental." (E. W. Brown.) In 1909, 1919, and 1928, William H. Pickering published his own predictions of a trans-Neptunian planet. His predicted orbit turned out to be even more in error than Lowell's. Yet: "Four photographic images of Pluto were obtained at Mount Wilson in 1919 during a search according to his directions, but somehow they went unnoticed. Incredible as it may seem, this prediction was also chance."[151]

Here is an arresting quotation from a book called *The World of Ted Serios,* by Jule Eisenbud, M.D.: "I think the supposition that we are finally forced to face as probably the most plausible is that [psi power] is 'manifest,' but in ways that our conventional categories of thought do not favor our being able easily to discern. . . . the insight I am leading up to . . . is, of course, that the latent mental power which all of us possess goes into sustaining—and is thus manifest in—all the natural processes that we see around us, from the growth of the lowliest seed to the movements of the heavenly bodies. It might thus be put down under the heading of 'general maintenance.'"

I give this at some length in order to say, with due caution and with certain reservations, that I don't believe in it. It has a certain loony logic, and it is attractive to think that Pluto may not have been discovered until 1930, not because it is so far away, but because it wasn't there until astronomers started looking for it. . . . But this would mean we would have to suppose that when the majority of men thought the stars were in crystal spheres rotating about the Earth, and so on. And then there are difficulties: when the Europeans thought the world was round and the Indians thought it was flat, was it round in Europe and flat in India?

A graver objection is that from a cosmic viewpoint this is such a parochial idea: it would mean that the whole starry universe depends on our belief in it, whereas the inhabitants of other stars have no such power over us. I can see a possible way out of this difficulty, however: Except for a few Greek philosophers, nobody believed that planets of other stars were inhabited until a few centuries ago. Nowadays many people believe it, and therefore it is true; and consequently we have dreamed something into existence which limits our power to dream.

Well, this may be the answer after all, and if so, it will be proved to be the answer when men believe in it; and when they don't believe in it, it will be proved not to be the answer.

In any event, there are hints of an elusive pattern in the *kinds* of things that fall. Why should they be frogs, lizards, fish—why not rains of turnips, or grapes, or oranges? When things fall from the sky which are not products of nature, but manufactured articles, why should they be bullets and nails? Why not paper clips, or erasers? Stones, bullets, nails that rattle from roofs . . . these are missiles, things snatched up to be thrown. Erasers, perhaps, would not rattle so satisfactorily.

And then the strange suggestion, in some of these accounts, that things happen as if in an attempt to explain other things that happen. . . . Or clumsy imitations: a chimney cleaned, dislodging soot, and then flows of soot; an accidental fire, and then impossible fires. A suggestion of mind at work, but a childish mind.

When we are dealing with things that happen in a single household, it is comforting to think that they are caused by the demanding, violent, irrational unconscious mind of an adolescent. But when fish rain over a whole town, or when red dust falls over half Europe, or when strange lights in the sky are seen by thousands, are we to suppose that we have to do with a *collective* dementia?

Perhaps we give ourselves too much credit. Perhaps

our minds are only something like radio beacons. Perhaps strange things are reported chiefly from inhabited places, not merely because there is no one in uninhabited places to report them, but because things do not happen in uninhabited places. Human minds, in certain states of high irritability and anxiety . . . do they distort the space-time frame around them, forming the narrow end of a funnel in four-space, down which things clatter and tumble? Think not only of poltergeists, but of the strange lights in the sky seen in Wales in 1905. This was a time of the most intense religious enthusiasm in Wales. Is there a polarity of madness, and do certain kinds of irrational states attract irrational happenings, not related to them except in being irrational?

If there is a universal mind, must it be sane?

Fort has some provocative notes on hatred. A wave of unexplained mansion fires, in England, in 1926—thirty in about ten months. In 1922 and 1923 explosions of coal in England and on the Continent. Coal, British coal, was exploding in grates, in stoves, in buckets. People were killed, houses demolished. It was suggested that the underpaid British miners were putting dynamite into coal; but none was ever found, and no coal exploded in shipment.

Then there was the case of John Blackman, also in 1922. Blackman, a labor leader in Eastbourne, was sent to jail for nonsupport of his wife. The judge who sentenced him died suddenly. When Blackman got out, he still refused to pay, so back he went. The judge who sentenced him died suddenly. Twice more he was sent back to jail, and twice more the judge who sentenced him "died suddenly."

From December, 1967, to March, 1968, there was an

extraordinary wave of fires and explosions, concurrently with a series of disasters to military aircraft, ships, and submarines. I have notes of twenty of the latter, including the crash of a B-52 carrying hydrogen bombs in Greenland, the disappearance of the Israeli submarine *Dakar* and the French submarine *Minerve* in the same week, and the capture of the United States intelligence ship *Pueblo* by the North Koreans. In January the United States nuclear sub *Seawolf* was damaged when it struck the ocean floor off the Atlantic coast. In February a Navy rescue ship was accidentally sunk by a Bullpup missile from an A-4 Skyhawk Navy aircraft; a United States reconnaissance plane on a training flight disappeared over South Korea; an Army helicopter on a training flight crashed near Savannah, Georgia; and a Navy T-33 jet trainer crashed into the San Francisco-Oakland Bay Bridge.

I think of the collective fear and hatred felt by millions of people toward machines of war, particularly those of the United States. And then the stories of explosions, which always end laconically, "The cause has not been determined." I have a note of one that destroyed a house in Riverdale, New York, a prosperous suburb of New York City. Living in the house were two policemen. A third policeman was bitten by a dog while leading the residents of the house next door to safety.

Flows of soot, and fish, and stones. . . . Flows of lymph and blood in a human body. . . . Do things fall where a universal mind, which may be the mind of an idiot, conceives that they are needed? When fish fall, is it because there are thoughts of hunger, and when blood flows from statues, is it because there are thoughts of blood? When stones fall, is it because there are thoughts of violence? When fires consume old women, is it because there are thoughts of death and hellfire? If so, when we are old, let us take care to think only nice, clean, benevolent thoughts.

Then there is "luck." An old friend of mine firmly believed that his luck was bad; and in fact his life was a series of disasters, punctuated by attempts at suicide. I cannot help believing that the disasters were suicidal too; that my friend deliberately, even if unconsciously, maneuvered himself into situations where disasters would have to happen. I also believe, although I can't possibly prove it, that my own life has been a series of maneuvered "accidents" of the other kind—lucky ones. Again and again I have done necessary things under strong compulsion, without knowing why. Only with hindsight can I see what the reasons were.

This is teleological thinking, and I know perfectly well that it is heretical. We are committed to the idea that the future cannot be known because it does not exist. Time, we say, is like a river on which we float—but what a peculiar river! Ahead of us, it does not yet exist; behind us, it no longer exists. A similar view of space might be that of the earthworm. Unable to perceive the earth ahead or behind, he might, if given to philosophical pursuits, believe that only "here" exists. In our superior wisdom, we would consider this presumptuous of the earthworm.

J. B. Priestley, in *Man and Time,* quotes from an article on "Precognition and Intervention," by Dr. Louisa E. Rhine, published in the *Journal of Parapsychology:*

> Many years ago when my son, who is now a man with a baby a year old, was a boy I had

a dream early one morning. I thought the children and I had gone camping with some friends. We were camped in such a pretty little glade on the shores of the sound between two hills. It was wooded, and our tents were under the trees. I looked around and thought what a lovely spot it was.

I thought I had some washing to do for the baby, so I went to the creek where it broadened out a little. There was a nice clean gravel spot, so I put the baby and the clothes down. I noticed I had forgotten the soap so I started back to the tent. The baby stood near the creek throwing handfuls of pebbles into the water. I got my soap and came back, and my baby was lying face down in the water. I pulled him out but he was dead. I awakened then, sobbing and crying. What a wave of joy went over me when I realized that I was safe in bed and that he was alive. I thought about it and worried for a few days, but nothing happened and I forgot about it.

During that summer some friends asked the children and me to go camping with them. We cruised along the sound until we found a good place for our camp near fresh water. The lovely little glade between the hills had a small creek and big trees to pitch our tents under. While sitting on the beach with one of the other women watching the children play one day, I happened to think I had some washing to do, so I took the baby and went to the tent for the clothes. When I got back to the creek I put down the baby and the clothes, and then I

> noticed that I had forgotten the soap. I started back for it, and as I did so, the baby picked up a handful of pebbles and threw them in the water. Instantly my dream flashed into my mind. It was like a moving picture. He stood just as he had in my dream—white dress, yellow curls, shining sun. For a moment I almost collapsed. Then I caught him up and went back to the beach and my friends. When I composed myself, I told them about it. They just laughed and said I imagined it. That is such a simple answer when one cannot give a good explanation. I am not given to imagining wild things.

Two comments need to be made about this account: first, that it is a common human experience, and second, that it involves a paradox. As Priestley points out: "This leaves us with a future already existing so that it can be discovered by one part of the mind, and with a future that can be shaped by the exercise of our free will."[152] Or: if the baby *did not drown,* because of the mother's precognitive vision, how could she have had the vision that he *had* drowned?

It is clear that one "time" is not enough to explain events like this. J. W. Dunne, in *An Experiment With Time,* proposed a second time dimension, "Time 2," in which the consciousness of the dreamer is able to survey Time 1; and a Time 3, in which he is able to survey Time 2, and so on. But this is unsatisfactory because it leads to an infinite regress. Priestley himself inclines toward the notion that time branches at every point of accident or decision. This has the disadvantage that it seems to involve the *creation* of a new time track by the conscious decision of the man confronted with a choice. It is perhaps easier to believe that all possible universes coexist, side by side, in a five-dimensional space-time framework.

The British astronomer Fred Hoyle explores this possibility in a book called *October the First Is Too Late.* The book is fiction, but Hoyle says pointedly, in a note to the reader, that the discussions of the meaning of time and of consciousness are meant seriously.

Hoyle's spokesman in the novel begins by saying that the experience of time as an "ever-rolling stream" is an illusion, and that "if there's one thing we can be sure about in physics it is that all times exist with equal reality. If you consider the motion of the Earth around the Sun, it is a spiral in four dimensional space-time. There's absolutely no question of singling out a special point on the spiral and saying that particular point is the present position of the Earth. Not so far as physics is concerned."[153]

He goes on to explain his idea of time by means of a metaphor: a wall of pigeonholes, millions of them, or an infinite number if you like, all arranged in numerical sequence. Each pigeonhole represents a moment of consciousness: each contains a story on a little slip of paper, and when the stories are read in sequence, they form the orderly progression of events as we experience it. But each pigeonhole also contains statements about the stories to be found in other pigeonholes; and if you examine these, you find a curious thing. The statements about stories in earlier pigeonholes are substantially correct; the statements about later ones are fuzzy, inaccurate, often completely wrong. It is this gradient of *information* that governs the sequence of the pigeonholes, and that gives us the illusion that the future is unknowable because it "does not yet exist."

Now we are asked to imagine that a clerk is looking into one pigeonhole after another, in no particular order. As the clerk's light falls into each pigeonhole, your consciousness is illuminated. But even though he looks into pigeonhole 137, then pigeonhole 2, then pigeonhole 1,983, and so on, the information gradient between the pigeonholes causes you to experience them as an orderly sequence.

What is the light that shines into the pigeonholes? Hoyle suggests that it is a superconsciousness, able to dip into the mind of any creature that has existed or will exist. In effect, we are all one.

This idea has another consequence, that death is an illusion. To begin with, when a man "dies," his consciousness does not vanish: it is still there, in the pigeonholes, to be illuminated millions of times, or an infinite number of times. Secondly, suppose a set of circumstances in which it is equally likely that a man will live or die. Hoyle puts this in terms of a doomsday machine, set to destroy all life on Earth *if* a particular atomic nucleus decays within a given period of a few seconds.

"'Do we all survive or don't we? My guess is that inevitably we appear to survive, because there is a division, the world divides into two, into two completely disparate stacks of pigeonholes. In one, a nucleus undergoes decay, explodes the bomb, and wipes us out. But the pigeonholes in that case never contain anything further about life on the Earth. So although those pigeonholes might be activated, there could never be any awareness that an explosion had taken place. In the other block, the Earth would be safe, our lives would continue —to put it in the usual phrase. Whenever the spotlight of consciousness hit those pigeonholes we should be aware of the Earth and we should decide the bomb had not exploded.' "[154]

I suspect that most people, if anyone bothered to ask, would say they have survived experiences that should have killed them. A friend of mine, an electrician, was doing some work on the exterior of a house when his ladder slipped; to save himself, he instinctively grabbed a high-tension power line. He felt the surge of current into his body, and smelled his skin burning. He should not have been able to open his hand; but he did, and survived.

Fort says, in *Many Parts:* "[We] three found an old revolver of large caliber; snapping the rusty, old revolver at one another. Just happening to aim at something else when it went off; nothing left of the something else. Slipping on roofs, but catching a projection just before going over. Beams and stones falling in the Capitol just where we had been a second before. Run over more than once, we lying quiet between wheels or runners. Breaking through the ice; someone throwing a skate strap to us. Here we are still. That in all this world there should be more than two or three grown men seems remarkable."[155]

If Hoyle is right, accidents and disease cannot kill us: when one track stops, our consciousness simply continues on another.

If there are alternate Earths, only minutely different from one another, there is no reason to suppose they are "stacked" in a rectilinear array; they may be skewed in time—as if someone had put his hand on a stack of film strips and pushed with gentle pressure, so that the top strip slid forward a little, the next a little less, and so on. (I borrow this image from a novel by James Blish, *Jack of Eagles,* which will be mentioned again in chapter eleven.) There might be a difference of months or years between adjacent worlds—and Louisa Rhine 1 might dream of Louisa Rhine 2 finding her child drowned in the creek.

One famous series of experiments apparently demonstrated that telepathy is possible between identical twins. In instances of "precognition" are we dealing with telepathy between two people who are *closer* than identical twins?

Consider now the phenomenon of the "green thumb" in chemical engineering. Ted Thomas, a chemical engineer and a patent attorney for Armstrong Cork Company, has written about this: he says it is known to every chemical engineer but rarely talked about. When a company licenses a new process and sets it up for the first time, again and again it will happen that although instructions have been followed to the letter, the process won't work. It will continue not to work, no matter how many times it is tried or how diligently the causes of failure are searched for, until someone who has previously performed the operation comes and leads the engineer in charge through the process once. After that the new man can do it himself. Nobody knows why.

Thomas also says that the examples given in chemical patents are a standing joke among chemical engineers; it is almost always impossible to duplicate them on the first try. "The guy who's lived with it can do it, and the stranger cannot, not until he's done enough work on it to have the *feel.*" But what do we mean by the "feel"?

The influence of experimenters' expectations has been studied by Robert Rosenthal of Harvard and Lenore Jacobson of the South San Francisco Unified School District. Their 1967 report has the pregnant title "Self-

Fulfilling Prophecies in the Classroom: Teachers' Expectations as Unintended Determinants of Pupils' Intellectual Competence."

All the children in the Oak School, in the San Francisco area, were given a test which purported to predict academic "blooming" or intellectual growth; actually, the test was a standard IQ test, Flanagan's Tests of General Ability. In the fall of 1964 the teachers in the Oak School were given a list of names, comprising about 20 percent of the students, and were told that these were the students who had scored high on the test and would therefore be "academic spurters" during the coming year. Actually, the students' names had been selected by means of a table of random numbers. Four months later, and again after another four months, the children were given the same test.

The results showed that although there was no significant difference between the two groups in the upper four grades of Oak School, in the two lowest grades the selected children had fulfilled their teachers' expectations. In the first grade, children of the experimental group gained over 15 IQ points more than the children in the control group. In the second grade, children of the experimental group gained nearly 10 points more than children in the control group. In the first and second grades combined, 19 percent of the control group children gained 20 or more IQ points. Among the experimental group, 47 percent gained 20 or more points.

The interpretation of these results is not entirely clear. It does not seem that the teachers spent more time with the children in the experimental group. If this had been the case, they would necessarily have spent less time with the control-group children, "robbing Peter to pay Paul." In that event, it would be expected that gains made by experimental-group children would be negatively correlated with gains made by control-group children—the more the experimental group gained, the less the control group would have gained. On the contrary, the results showed a positive correlation, large and statistically significant.

The authors suggest that the children may have been encouraged by unconscious cues given by the teacher—her facial expressions, the tone of her voice, and so on; but they conclude that more study is needed to establish this.

In a previous study, Rosenthal performed the same sort of experiment on rats. One group of experimenters was told that their rats had been especially bred for brilliance; the other group, that their rats were genetically inferior and should not be expected to perform well. Actually, the rats were from the same strain and were assigned to the experimenters at random. As in the Oak School experiment, the rats fulfilled the experimenters' expectations.

In this case, the unconscious-cue theory seems a little suspect. Rosenthal suggests that supposedly bright rats may have been handled more, and more gently, by the experimenter. Again, data on this point is lacking.

The next step, which has not been taken by anyone as far as I can find out, would be to make a similar study of experiments involving chemical reactions. In order to control all variables except experimenter expectation, a moderately complex and difficult chemical process should be automated. One group of experimeters should be told that their reagents are of exceptional purity; the other group, that they will be working with impure reagents. If the results should show a significant difference in the results obtained by the two groups, that would be very interesting.

Chapter Ten

Forces Are Moving Me (1920–1932)

Something has isolated me, and mostly it has been because I have put in my time as a writer of treatments and subjects with which the world would have nothing to do. In earlier times I often got drunk about this, but I am not resentful now. The world has cut me out for the very good reason that I have cut myself out. . . . I am not misanthropic: I have considerable liking for people, so long as I can keep away from them.

A Book About Caiques, by Charles Fort (unpublished manuscript)

Charles Hoy Fort, aged forty-six, went on with his yarns. In 1920 he wrote to Dreiser that he had been keeping a copy of *The Book of the Damned* for him, hoping he would drop in, but now gave it up, because he was going to drop out. He went on:

> Forces are moving me. I've cut ties with Albany, and published in the "Tribune" my dissatisfaction with the New York Public Library, so that I can't very comfortably go back there, and have burned all my notes, 40,000 of them. Forces are moving me to London. Annie and I sail on the 27th. I hope you'll always write to me, once a year, c/o Messrs. Brown, Shipley & Co., 123 Pall Mall, London, SW. I have burned and destroyed and cut, but I have kept some letters—and may strange orthogenetic gods destroy me if I ever forget all that was done for me by Theodore Dreiser! I send a copy of "The B. of the D." in this mail.[156]

Fort and Anna took lodgings at 15 Marchmont Street, a few blocks from the British Museum. Fort settled into a routine: up at eight, work on his notes till lunchtime; off to the Museum at two, back at five. After supper, four or five times a week, he would take Anna to the movies; other evenings he went to Hyde Park, where he had found a congenial group of loungers to argue with. Said Anna, "Charlie left every night at nine when I came to meet him, after wandering around the park. The men used to make fun of him going home at nine, but he had had enough of it by this time. He liked solitude. . . . He did not want anyone to come in, and he did not want to go out."

In the evenings he read the latest chapters of his books to Anna. They quarreled sometimes over the marketing, about which Fort was very particular. "I remember," Anna said, "once in London I went to a delicatessen and paid a dollar a pound for something. He did not like delicatessen stuff anyway, but when I came back with this, he said, 'It's a damned shame, that's what it is, for you to bring in old, cheap stuff to me.' I said, 'I paid a dollar a pound for it,' but he did not believe it. I went to the delicatessen and got the bill. He apologized. He always thought I was doing him on the meat."

When they were in London, Anna said, Fort "used to stand in the street and gaze at the stars and point them out to me and tell me the meaning of it. Then up in our rooms he would throw open the windows and stand gazing at the stars. That was his delight for a long, long time."[157]

In January, 1921, Fort wrote to Raymond and his family:

> Ray, Tess, Harriet:
>
> Thank you for your cards, which we received a little late, but not so late as, according to my fears, your next cards may be. What do you know but that I've heard some talk of taking my stuff seriously—somebody may organize an expedition to the Moon, to find out what there is in these things I'm writing about—and I'll have to go along—how can I get out of going!
>
> England seems some distance—but I have an awful suspicion that I'll be up in the moon, next Christmas. Of course I'll take Annie with me—[158]

Fort and Anna spent six months in England, then returned to New York. In December, 1921, they were back in London, this time at 39 Marchmont Street, a few doors away from their previous address, over a fruiterer's. In April, 1922, Fort sent Dreiser a fairy cross with a note: "See *Book of the Damned,* p. 159." Another fairy cross, which he sent Dreiser in 1930, is still in the folded letter at the University of Pennsylvania Library, and I have seen it: it is a beautiful little thing, a perfectly formed cross of brown stone about half an inch long.

The writer Miriam Allen deFord has another of these crosses which Fort sent her in the thirties. Miss deFord's late husband, Maynard Shipley, a writer and critic, corresponded with Fort in the twenties and thirties; it was he who wrote, reviewing *Lo!* in the New York *Times,* "To read Charles Fort is to ride on a comet!"

The Shipleys had come across *The Book of the Damned* in a lending library in 1921, and had sat up all night, reading it aloud to each other, unable to put it down.

> My husband . . . was about equally impressed by the mass of data and outraged by some of the rash conclusions drawn from them. He wrote to the author, in care of the publisher, and told him so. After a long time an answer came from London, where Charles Fort was gathering more "damned facts" in the British Museum. That was the beginning of a correspondence which lasted until Fort's death in 1932. We never met in person, but we became good friends on paper—which to a shy, introverted man like Fort was much more desirable, anyway, than any face-to-face encounters. In 1922 there was a celebrated series of stone-falls at Chico, California. I went there and investi-

gated it for Fort, and myself saw a stone fall from some invisible point in the sky and land gently at my feet.[159] The questions Fort asked me and the care he took in getting details straight taught me something of his obstinate search for verification—a search so intensive that for several years it cost him his sight.

Though great reputations and established systems scared him not at all, Charles Fort was the least dogmatic of men. The last thing he wanted was to set himself up as a dictator or a pundit. He knew very well that his function was to act as a gadfly on the hide of orthodox science, to sting it awake. In the letter he sent us with a presentation copy of *Lo!* he said: "Maybe it's awful. Maybe somebody had to do it. Maybe it was just my luck to be picked out." Of one of his other books he remarked wryly that perhaps it was "a sanitarium for overworked coincidences."[160]

Another early admirer of Fort's was the science fiction writer Edmond Hamilton, who began corresponding with him in the twenties and wrote two Fort-inspired short stories. One of these, "The Earth Owners,"[161] has been called the first Fortean s.f. story, but Hamilton himself notes that it was preceded by George Allan England's "The Thing From Outside."[162]

In May, 1926, Fort wrote from London:

It is quite as you say—poor old Theology hammered all around, but Science the great Immune. And, so far as I know, mine are about the only books of impoliteness to scientific dogmas written by one who has not the theological bias. Every now and then I get a letter from somebody who thinks I am some kind of a Fundamentalist, simply because I don't take in, without questioning, everything that the scientists tell us: but I think I made it plain in the books that I am not out to restore Moses.

I think that your clippings are remarkable for so short a period. I never heard of deep-buried, living oysters before, but I have notes upon about a hundred other living things said to have been found alive in ancient rocks.

I am very glad to know of your interest in the subject, but that we shall ever organize does not seem likely to me. I think I told you that the idea is not mine, but was tried, without success, several years ago, by Mr. J. D. Stern, editor of the Camden (N.J.) "Daily Courier." The great trouble is that the majority of persons who are attracted are the ones that we do not want; Spiritualists, Fundamentalists, persons who are revolting against Science, not in the least because they are affronted by the myth-stuff of the sciences, but because scientists either oppose or do not encourage them. I accept, myself, that there are psychic phenomena, and I think that Daniel Home, for instance, did have occult powers; but psychic phenomena and occult powers, and alleged communications with the dead, are in very different categories, in my view.[163]

Later that year Hamilton sent him some material about newspaper reports of "a Princeton geology prof. who on a field trip in Arizona had found inexplicable living frogs in a small pool of water in the burning desert . . . I wrote this geologist and he answered courteously but said it was absolutely impossible they could have fallen from the sky."[164]

Fort replied:

> Like you, I notice the learned gentleman's use of the word "absolutely." If he could apply that word to anything, say to a frog, that Frog would be God.
>
> Nevertheless—with the absoluteness left out—he may be right. It seems that those Arizona frogs were adults. There may have been showers of adult frogs, but in my records, of about 80 instances, all showering frogs were little ones. . . .[165]

In *Wild Talents,* which deals with extraordinary abilities of human beings, Fort wrote: "I have had what I think is about the average experience with magic." One evening in March, 1924, he was reading in the kitchen of his London flat when he heard a thump. A picture had fallen off the wall. The glass had not broken, because the picture had fallen on a pile of magazines. The next morning he got around to looking at it, and found that one of the brass rings on the back of the picture frame was broken in two places. Anna reminded him that two pictures had fallen recently in the flat above. Fort wrote: "The picture was not heavy. The look is that there had been a sharp, strong pull on the picture cord, so doubly to break this ring."

Six days later, sitting in the corner where the picture had fallen, he heard a crash of glass. "It was so sharp and loud that for hours afterward I had a sense of alertness to dodge missiles. It was so loud that Mrs. C., upstairs, heard it." But no glass had broken.

Ten days went by. On the morning of March 28, Fort found a second picture on the floor in the same corner. It had fallen from a place about three feet above the bureau on which he kept his boxes of notes. It was clear that it had not fallen in the ordinary way, or it would have hit the boxes, and there would have been "a heartbreaking mess" of notes on the floor. Among these notes, for whatever that may mean, were accounts of pictures unaccountably falling from walls.

Again, the glass was not broken. This time it was the picture cord that had parted. Fort tied a knot in it, and replaced the picture. It was a strong cord; Fort tried to break it by tugging at it, and could not. The nail that supported it showed no sign of strain.

On April 18 Anna reached for a picture, meaning to take it down and wash the glass, and it seemed to fall into her hands. She said, "Another picture cord rotten." Then, "No, the nail came out." Fort went and looked: the cord had not broken, and the nail was still in the wall. Later that day, Anna remarked, "I don't understand how that picture came down."

In October of that year, Fort made this note:

> . . . I was in the front room, thinking casually of the pictures that fell from the walls. This evening, my eyes bad. Unable to read. Was sitting, staring at the kitchen wall, fiddling with a piece of string. Anything to pass away time. I was staring right at a picture above corner of bureau, where the notes are, but having no consciousness of the picture. It fell. It hit boxes of

notes, dropped to floor, frame at a corner broken, glass broken.

The cord was broken several inches from one of the fastenings on back of picture. But there should have been this fastening, a dangling piece of cord, several inches long. This missing. I can't find it.

Pictures continued to fall; then they stopped. On November 3, 1926, Fort wrote in his notes that for more than a year no picture had fallen.

On the next day:

Nov. 4, 1926—This is worth noting. Last night, I noted about the pictures, because earlier in the evening, talking over psychic experiences with France and others, I had mentioned falling pictures in our house. Tonight, when I came home, *A* [Anna] told me of a loud sound that had been heard, and how welcome it was to her, because it had interrupted *E* [the neighbor upstairs], in a long tiresome account of the plot of a moving picture. Later, *A* exclaimed: "Here's what made the noise!" She had turned on the light, in the front room, and on the floor was a large picture. I had not mentioned to *A* that yesterday my mind was upon falling pictures. I took that note after she had gone to bed. I looked at the picture—cord broken, with frayed ends. I have kept a loop of this cord. The break is under a knot in it. Nov. 5—I have not strongly enough emphasized *A*'s state of mind, at the time of the fall of the picture. *E*'s long account of a movie had annoyed her almost

> beyond endurance, and probably her hope for an interruption was keen.

In *Wild Talents,* after quoting this passage, Fort added: "Here is an admission that I did not think, or suspect, that it was I, who was the magician, this time."

There was one later episode.

In October, 1929, the Forts were living in New York, "or, anyway, in the Bronx." In this flat there were no pictures on walls, although Fort later got some.

> October 5, 1929–I was looking over these notes, and I called *A* from the kitchen to discuss them. I note that *A* had been doing nothing in the kitchen. She had just come in: had gone to the kitchen to see what the birds were doing. While discussing those falling pictures, we heard a loud sound. Ran back, and found on the kitchen floor a pan that had fallen from a pile of utensils in a closet.
>
> October 18, 1930–I made an experiment. I read these notes aloud to *A,* to see whether there would be a repetition of the experience of Oct. 15, 1929. Nothing fell.
>
> Nov. 19, 1931–tried that again. Nothing moved. Well, then, if I'm not a wizard, I'm not going to let anybody else tell me that he's a wizard.[166]

On November 6, 1929, Fort noted in his journal that after the Wall Street crash he had sold twelve thousand dollars in bonds and reinvested seventy-five hundred in "highly speculative" stocks. He was financially secure, but felt that his writing career was over. He wrote, "I think that I, too, am coming to an end. My general health is very good, but I am almost blind in the right eye, and the left eye is going. I have gone over my papers, & sorted them, and packed away all my notes, as if quite clearly understanding that my time is coming. I can not stand living in blindness. I have made arrangements for Annie. Ten months ago, I read what I consider my last book. I have not had a library book since. Ten months ago the library work that was my life stopped, on acct. of eye trouble. . . . Two years ago, largely because of feeling of eye strain, I started the chrs. interest. This is all that I have now, and it looks as if at last I am specializing."

"Chrs." refers to Super-checkers, a game of Fort's invention. It was played with armies of men on a board with thousands of squares; Fort used bits of cardboard with carpet-tack handles for the men, and a piece of checkered cloth for the board. In 1930 he wrote to Tiffany Thayer: "Super-checkers is going to be a great success. I have met four more people who consider it preposterous."

He explained the rules in a letter to Edmond Hamilton. To begin the game, the two players, A and B, arranged their forces in oblong formations, with a space between, or in any other desired formation; a favorite of Fort's was two wedges, meeting at their points. Combat might begin at the point of contact, or the players might send out flanking movements. Since the game could go on continuously for a week if the players moved only one man at a time, it was best to move them *en masse*. "So let A start out, moving until B tells him to stop—say a hundred moves. Then B makes a hundred moves. A may want to make another hundred moves, but B, sizing up the situation, tells him to stop, say at thirty.

Then perhaps occurs 'fighting,' at close quarters, one move at a time, as in ordinary checkers. But, at any time, if either player wants to make a 'mass movement' that is a matter of obtaining permission from his opponent."[167]

Even with these improvements, a game of Superchekers usually lasted all night.

After reading *New Lands* in 1923, a young man named Tiffany Thayer wrote a letter of praise to Fort, mentioning Ben Hecht's remark that "five out of six persons who read this book will go mad." Fort replied: "Dear Sir: Ben Hecht is pretty good sometimes, but I do not think much of him as an alienist. According to my own researches, five out of every five persons are crazy in the first place." This was the beginning of a correspondence that continued until Fort came back to America to stay in 1929. In May, 1930, Fort invited Thayer to visit him in his Bronx apartment, and from then until Fort's death the two men were close friends.

Tiffany Ellsworth Thayer was born in Freeport, Illinois, in 1902, the son of Elmer Ellsworth Thayer and Sybil Madelin Thayer, both professional actors. Thayer himself went on the stage when he was fifteen, and for years used the name Elmer Ellsworth, Jr., even when he abandoned an unsuccessful career as an actor and went into advertising.

Thayer had been a reporter for a time in Chicago, then had managed a bookstore; he had gone into ad writing in 1926, and in 1930 was advertising manager for the Literary Guild at the Paul Mathewson Agency. An associate of his at Mathewson, Aaron Sussman, had formed a partnership with a rather dubious publisher named Claude Kendall, and the firm published Thayer's first novel, *Thirteen Men.* Thayer knew that Fort had an unpublished manuscript, and urged him to offer it to Sussman. Sussman liked the book; he did not like Fort's title, however, which was *Skyward Ho!* ("Books on aviation are not selling," Thayer wrote to Fort in August, 1930; "most folks work out their air-mindedness at two cents a copy each evening in the newspapers.")[168] Sussman suggested *God Is an Idiot,* but Fort did not care for that. Other suggestions were made, and nobody liked them.

Fort wrote to Thayer, "Good God—or Godness—or whatever it is—the people downstairs had a baby, and they simply named her Madeline, and there wasn't any argument. Still, I do admit that they're not trying to sell their brat."

Finally Thayer suggested *Lo!*—"because in the text the astronomers are forever calculating and then pointing to the sky where they figure a new star or something should be and saying 'Lo!'—and there's nothing whatever to be seen where they point."[169] Fort agreed immediately.

Sussman, who is now the head of Sussman & Sugar, Inc., an ad agency specializing in book advertising, vividly recalls his visits to Fort's apartment in 1930. Anna kept parakeets; she was "a bustling, militant little hostess"; she had "a lovely way of speaking to you—she made you feel she was honored and grateful that you had taken the time and trouble to come and see her." She adored Fort, and it was impossible not to like her; Sussman calls her "one of the most innocent innocents I have ever met." Fort himself was good-natured and convivial, "a very gentle man, inveterately polite, very tender toward Anna, most solicitous and concerned." He had a deep voice and a booming laugh. He impressed Sussman as like Schweitzer or Einstein—withdrawn from the world, but enormously affectionate and interested in other people. "He always made you feel wanted; he was delighted to see you, no matter how busy he was."

Thayer has described the Forts' Bronx apartment at 2051 Ryer Avenue. "On the walls of the flat were framed specimens of giant spiders, butterflies, weird creatures adept at concealment, imitating the sticks and leaves to which they were affixed. There was also framed a photograph of a baseball beside a hailstone, both objects the same size, sent to Fort by a correspondent, and—under glass—a specimen of some stuff that looks like dirty, shredded asbestos which had fallen from the sky in quantities covering several acres."[170]

Fort worked in a small, dark room overlooking a courtyard; it contained an old oak desk, a typewriter, a bookcase, and a stack of cardboard boxes filled with notes. After a morning spent in the library, he usually worked here until five. Four or five times a week, he and Anna went to the movies after supper. His favorite actress was Lillian Gish; but when he met her in Dreiser's home, according to Anna, he thought her "just ordinary." He liked Jack Holt, an actor who specialized in he-man roles, but most of the films he saw "bored him to death";[171] he went to keep Anna company.

Lo! was published in January, 1931, with illustrations by Alexander King, and Thayer seized the opportunity to announce the formation of the Fortean Society, at a dinner at the Savoy-Plaza on January 26. Present were Dreiser, Hecht, Burton Rascoe, J. Donald Adams, J. David Stern (publisher of the Philadelphia *Record*), Claude Kendall, and Aaron Sussman. Also present was Charles Fort, who had absolutely refused to have anything to do with the scheme and was lured to the hotel by mendacious telegrams. (In November he had written to Dreiser,

"About Ellsworth [Thayer], it is this—he is a good fellow, who is trying to limelight me, because he read me first when he was about twenty years old, and thinks he owes me a lot for it. He has gone to much trouble, for nothing. I told him that what he is trying to do might go some place, such as Orange, New Jersey. . . . As you know, I had nothing to do with this plan. I wouldn't join it, any more than I'd be an Elk.")[172]

The purposes of the Fortean Society, as set forth by Thayer at various times, were: to perpetuate the name of Charles Fort and promote the reading of his books; to preserve Fort's notes and papers; to continue the work of gathering Fortean data; and to encourage dissent.

The Society met irregularly, sometimes at members' homes and sometimes at a Yorkville restaurant, the Brauhaus, where the beer was as good as the talk. Thayer presided and usually led the discussions; Fort, who had steadfastly refused to join any organization named after him, played a minor role.

In March, in a letter that I find prophetic, Fort wrote to Maynard Shipley:

> My dear Shipley:
>
> I have read your review, and it is very encouraging to me. I note that you speak of my "daring." Yours is a higher type than mine. In writing one of my books, I risk nothing but the trouble in finding a publisher. This time, I had none, though an earlier version of "Lo!" travelled around unavailingly three or four years.
>
> Your review strengthens my notions of science as a system. How is it that you are not Prof. Shipley, snugly salaried and nested? The answer is that Prof. Shipley would be somebody

who could not see of one book, nor of anything else, so many aspects, at one time, as you see of "Lo!" He could see only what would fit him in snugly somewhere.

Something that you see in "Lo!" is that it is a kind of non-fictional fiction, or that, though concerned with entomological and astronomical matters, and so on, it is "thrilling" and "melodramatic." I have a theory that the moving pictures will pretty nearly drive out the novel, as they have very much reduced the importance of the stage—but that there will arise writing that will retain the principles of dramatic structure of the novel, but, not having human beings for its characters, will not be producable in the pictures, and will survive independently. Maybe I am a pioneer in a new writing that instead of old-fashioned heroes and villains, will have floods and bugs and stars and earthquakes for its characters and motifs.

I am very much encouraged with your review, the spirit of which is—discount what you will, something remains, just the same.[173]

Early in 1932 Fort's health began to fail, but he managed to complete the book he was working on, *Wild Talents,* and turn it in to Kendall. On the little slips of paper he used for all his notes, he kept a record of the progress of his illness.[174]

Feb. 13 I have been half dead—so weak couldn't go out walking, or felt weak walking a *little,* before today. Sat for first time & read, today.

Feb. 19 Without being definitely ill I can't take walks. Can't smoke half as much—have cut down meals one half—am sleeping poorly, have cut down beer. On "Wild Talents" I can do only 4, 5, or 6 pages a day.

Feb. 20 Finished "W.T." today. I can't write more than mornings, but I don't see that my writing abilities are affected.

Feb. 20 Me and my ailments? Annie just came to me & said: "Did you hear that?" "No" "Not the loud crash?" Later while at dinner 2 more packages of sugar fell—"supplies" sugar.

Feb. 23 Going to Loew's last night, I could not keep up, or nearly up, to Annie's pace.

Feb. 26 New difficulty, in shaving—gaunt places in my face.

Here the notes end.

Anna told Dreiser: "One time it was his habit to get through about five, but when he was working on *Wild Talents,* he had only a certain length of time to finish, and he worked himself to death. Sometimes he worked until it was time to go to the movies. Sometimes I would even go to the pictures alone, and he would follow. Then he could not go any more. . . . The last couple of weeks when he was sick, the landlord's son-in-law and daughter came up, and he didn't want to see anyone. I couldn't say, don't come in, so I took them into the dining room, and they stayed and had a glass of beer, and when they went, he said, 'Can't you cut out your afternoon entertainments?' I said, 'It is a very poor sort of entertainment, and I did it to save you.' Then there was an old lady who used to come up Saturday nights. He said not to let her come, that she was keeping me away from him. I said, 'I'll be in with you every ten minutes.' One night he was lying in bed. I was sitting outside. He said, 'Who have you got there?' I said, 'I haven't got a living soul; I am all alone.' And he was pleased that I had no one with me. He just wanted me—him and Momma—and no one else."

Fort would not see a doctor, but on the morning of May 3 he was so weak that Anna called an ambulance and had him taken to Royal Hospital. Sussman brought him advance copies of *Wild Talents*, but he could not lift his hand to take them. He died that day.[175]

Dreiser, in the interview quoted before, asked Anna if she had ever had any mysterious experiences. She told him of various rappings and voices; then this:

> One afternoon about eight months ago, his aunt came over, and she annoyed me terribly about this money. She said I had no right to it. I went to bed crying, and in the night I thought he was sitting on a little bench or couch which I have in the bedroom. He said, "Hello, Momma," and I was never so glad to see anybody in my whole life.

Charles Fort was buried in the family plot in Albany. Anna survived him by only five years. In her will she left bequests to Harvard and New York University, establishing funds to be used for grants to deserving students, in honor of her husband. She left small bequests to a number of friends and neighbors. The rest of her estate, including her interest in the estate of Peter V. Fort, still unsettled after all these years, went to Raymond Fort.

Chapter Eleven

Skyward Ho! (1935–1959 Old Style)

I am able to imagine an "Earth" which is a small ball of cosmic-ice, changing ever so slowly to a slightly larger cube of cosmic-ice, then "bursting" (hatching?) into a ball seven times as large as before, scratching whatever of the elements are within it to be scratched. (Luna, I think, is such an ice-ball today, and should be watched for the appearance of corners.)

Tiffany Thayer, in *Doubt,* number 39 (1952)

On February 26, 1935, Thayer wrote to Dreiser, on the Fortean Society letterhead:

Dear Dreiser:

For the first time since we founded this society, I have some leisure to devote to it. I have tried to think how our aims could be best

> served and I think the publication of a Fortean periodical is the first step. Through the columns of a magazine, interested persons, the members etc., could be kept in touch with each other and in it we could print Fort's notes in periodical slices—like a serial. Decyphering the cryptic shorthand of them, written in Fort's strange hand, is a tremendous undertaking but I am making headway and I will have a sufficient quantity transcribed by the time they will be needed for the magazine.
>
> It is my thought that the paper could be called nothing but THE FORTEAN. It is my idea to give it as much outward appearance of substantial popularity as possible, with your photograph on the cover and a lead article by you. If you can not provide the article at the moment, the lead article can be *about* you, establishing (our best foot forward) the type of intelligence Fort attracted, dwelling upon your own work and naming you as Fort's discoverer and the first friend of his genius.

Thayer went on to say that this seemed to him the only practical way to get the notes into print, since no publisher would touch them as a book. He added that he thought the notes ought to be available for the use of scholars, but that "for you or me or any of the group named on this page as founders of the society to attempt to develop that material in immitation [sic] of Fort would smack of ghoulishness. . . ."

This was an unfortunate choice of words. Dreiser replied on March 5 that he declined to have anything further to do with the Fortean Society. He was piqued about the notes, which Thayer had taken before he had had a chance to examine them. He said: "Incidentally, it strikes me as presumptuous and ungracious for the only person who seized upon his property and disappeared with it, to indulge in thought concerning ghoulishness of developing material in imitation of Fort. Exactly who would be mentally capable of imitating Charles Fort? I do not see any name on the list of founders that would be likely to achieve anything but a ridiculous imitation—nothing that would in any way interfere with the sound and just progress of his ultimate fame. The remarks are characteristic of your entire attitude in regard to me and this society, and as far as I am concerned I desire to have nothing more to do with this venture as it is at present constituted. If at some time the thing is shaped up in such a way as to make sure the real advancement of Fort's mental interests, I will be glad to do what I can. As it now stands I see nothing but a tentative adventure on your part looking to decidedly undefine [sic] purposes of your own."

Thayer's response to this opened with a classic understatement: "Now—look. You're just angry."[176] He explained, truthfully, that Fort before his death had given him a letter authorizing him to take possession of the notes; but Dreiser was not mollified. He answered:

> My dear Thayer:
>
> Your general procedure is egoistic and utterly inconsiderate of any desires or problems other than those that relate to yourself. Your whole course in connection with Fort and myself at least has indicated as much to me. I do not care to work with you. My decision is to remove my

> name from the Fortean Society and I hereby formally request you to do this at once.
>
> If, as an outsider, at some time or another I can be of service to the Society in connection with Fort and his material I will be glad, if possible, to be of such service.[177]

Thayer started the magazine anyway; the first issue of *The Fortean Society Magazine* appeared in September, 1937. Dreiser's picture was not on the cover, nor did his name appear, then or ever, in the list of the Founders which Thayer published in every issue. The lead article, written by Thayer, was headlined WHO KILLED EARHART AND NOONAN? The first paragraph gave his answer: "I won't be quiet—if this is the last collection of words I set down on paper—not if this is the last breath I draw. Amelia Earhart and Fred Noonan were murdered by Dogmatic Science." Thayer's reasoning appeared to be that if Dogmatic Science had been doing its job, the Earth would have been measured and mapped more accurately, and the two aviators would not have been lost.

In this issue Thayer began transcribing and publishing the notes of Charles Fort, an undertaking which he continued in installments throughout the life of the magazine. This was a major project, but Thayer characteristically made it sound more difficult than it was. The notes, he said, "were written in pencil—over a period of twenty-six years—in a code known only to the author—a sort of personal shorthand." The notes still exist; they are in Fort's idiosyncratic handwriting and include a number of abbreviations, but they are not in code or shorthand.

In early issues, Thayer made a conscientious effort to publish source material of a kind that might be expected to be of value to future Fortean investigators; the first issue, for example, carried a chart of "The Sky This Month" and a detailed September ephemeris; the second issue (October, 1937), a chart of the tides of New York harbor, as recorded by an automatic gauge at the foot of Whitehall Street, together with tides predicted by the United States Coast and Geodetic Survey. ("The chart is strictly for Forteans. It requires some concentration for its fullest enjoyment. All who are quite content with the explanation that 'the moon causes the tides' and are blissfully willing to leave the comprehension of that brash allegation to others are warned off. Run away, the chart will bite you.")

With the third issue (January, 1940), all this had disappeared. Eric Frank Russell, an enthusiastic Fortean, contributed frequent gleanings from the press, and managed the Society's affairs in England. Thayer continued to run reports of Fortean phenomena, as well as other news items that struck his fancy, but his major preoccupations became political. In the third issue, under the headline WE HAVE THE FREEDOM BUT WHERE'S THE PRESS?, he forecast the entry of the United States into the war and called it the result of the greatest propaganda campaign in history. "Tonight I am able to write these lines and tomorrow I may find a printer willing to print them if I can pay him. . . . In a few weeks—after war is declared—if I attempt to do any such thing I will be clapped in jail."

A year and four months later, still out of jail, he published the fourth issue, announcing Holt's publication of *The Books of Charles Fort.* In following issues, he continued to inveigh against the war ("The Great Hoax"), and against civil defense. In the seventh issue (June, 1943), he published a long list of Socratic questions—

one hundred and seventeen, minus a few marked "deleted on second thought." A sampling of these follows:

1. How long is an "emergency" and who says so?

2. Can New York City be bombed without the connivance of Washington, D.C.?

3. Does anybody still think this so-called "war" will ever be over?

5. Where was James A. Farley from July 27, 1939, until Sept. 2, 1939?

7. Did the then Chairman of the Republican National Committee (John D. M. Hamilton) visit Europe at the same time?

8. Did they both see Hitler or his agents?

In its eleventh issue (Winter, 1944–45), the magazine's name was changed to *Doubt,* subtitled *The Fortean Society Magazine.* Thayer published the magazine as a hobby, and made up its losses out of his own pocket. Fortean Society dues were never more than two dollars a year, and Thayer seldom or never dropped anybody for nonpayment.

In person, Thayer was an aggressive little man, contentious and rude. Faber Birren, an old friend, says he liked Thayer but could not stand his company for long at a time.

In his novel *Jack of Eagles,* James Blish, a Fortean Society member, described Thayer (thinly disguised as "Cartier Taylor") in the following terms:

> He viewed scientists-in-the-mass as a kind of priesthood, and scientific method as a new form of mumbo-jumbo. This twist made him partial to astrology, hollow-earth notions, Lemuria, pyramidology, phrenology, Vedanta, black magic,

> Koreshanity, Theosophy, Rosicrucianism, crystalline atoms, lunar farming, Atlantis, and a long list of similar asininities—the more asinine the better. At bottom, however, every one of these beliefs . . . turned out to rest on some form of personal-devil theory: Roosevelt had sold the world down the river, the world press was out to suppress reports of unorthodox happenings, astronomers conspired to wangle money for useless instruments, physicists were secretly planning to promote the purchase of cyclotrons by high schools, the Catholic Church was about to shut down independent thinking throughout the United States, doctors were promoting useless or dangerous drugs because they were expensive—all with the glossiest of plausible surfaces, all as mad as the maddest asylum-shuttered obsession of direct persecution.[178]

As editor of *Doubt,* Thayer took a perverse delight in encouraging cranks of all sorts. He published information about the "Cosmic Constant" of Frank S. Lonc (1.618+, a numerical relationship which according to its discoverer is found throughout the universe—e.g., when the distance from the crown of the head to the navel is taken as 1, the distance from the navel to the soles of the feet is found to be 1.618+); and the spheric space of Dr. Ernst Philipp Barthel (the Earth is the under-half of the universe). Thayer himself had a theory, which he mentioned in the first issue of *The Fortean Society Magazine* and elaborated later, that the Earth and all other planets are constantly growing by a method which entails sudden changes from the spherical to the cubical form, and back again.

He crusaded against vaccination, the fluoridation of drinking water, the needless removal of tonsils, the indiscriminate use of new wonder drugs; in some of these things, later events suggested that he had been right.

He supported those who refused induction into the armed services during the Korean War on the grounds that the war was undeclared and therefore illegal. He poked fun at astronomers. He suspected that "flying saucers" were an invention of the military to keep people's minds off their real problems, but patiently collected data on them anyhow, and printed a long summary of saucer reports in *Doubt*. He published newspaper clippings of Fortean events sent in by members, patiently urging them from time to time not to use Scotch tape or rubber cement, which made the data stick together. On the whole, he was good-humored; when he was shrill, he was too shrill to be taken seriously.

In the ninth issue, he announced the Society's adoption of a thirteen-month calendar. The additional month was called "Fort," and came between August and September. He noted regretfully that the inventor of the thirteen-month calendar, Moses B. Cotsworth, had died "June 4, 1943, old style," at the age of eighty-three. "Mr. Cotsworth's name for the 13th month was 'Sol,' but that was because the importance of Charles Fort had not been brought to his attention."

In issue 24 (April, 1949), Thayer ran pictures of four recently married couples who had met through the Society—Mr. and Mrs. Sam Youd, Mr. and Mrs. Kirk Drusai, Mr. and Mrs. G. C. Bump (I kid you not), and Mr. and Mrs. Vincent Gaddis. Gaddis is now a well-known writer of books on Fortean subjects; Youd is better known as the novelist John Christopher.

In the summer of 1952 Thayer and his wife went to

Europe, visited the Russells in England, and took a trip with them to Ireland, where Mrs. Thayer had distant relatives. According to Russell, "Thayer was as cynical about the F.S. as Fort was incredulous about himself. This was due, in part, to the fact that the F.S., by its nature, inevitably attracted more than its fair share of loonies. [Mrs. Thayer], as wives do, picked up some of this attitude and, when in Dublin, took delight in nudging Thayer, pointing out some cross-eyed, crazy-looking Irishman, and saying: 'There's a member—go get him!' "[179]

It was also on this European trip, apparently, that Thayer picked up the Fortean Society's only titled member, Prince Boris De Rachewiltz. In *Doubt*, number 38, along with pictures of the Thayers and Russells in Dublin, appear two views of Prince Boris's castle in the Italian Alps.

On his return, Thayer scored a moral victory over officialdom. As a matter of principle he and his wife had refused to be vaccinated, and accordingly they had no vaccination certificates. When the ship docked in New York, they were told they must be vaccinated or undergo fourteen days' quarantine. Thayer politely replied that vaccination was contrary to their religious principles, and that, in effect, if the ship's officers wanted to quarantine them, they could call the paddy wagon.

> After the ship was moored and the passengers all ashore, the first officer came to us and called YS to a table aside. The Superior Officer had not found sufficient evidence in our physical condition to warrant holding us in quarantine, he said, but he gave us a form on which he wrote a telephone number. As the price of obtaining our landing cards, YS had to promise to

call that number every day for eight days and report on the state of the Thayers' health.

That seemed reasonable enough, and so we left the ship, and we have called every day faithfully and said we felt fine and hoped they were the same.

Vive the Religion of Self Respect!

Dreiser died in 1945, aged seventy-four. In 1946 Thayer wrote to Helen Dreiser, in a letter dated "5/28/16 FS, 5/18/46 old style."

Dear Mrs. Theodore Dreiser:

Our good member, Mrs. Jennie S. Thomas, has sent us a letter which you wrote to her on April 30, in which you suggest that I address you, personally, with a view toward acquiring Mr. Dreiser's Fort material for the Society.

Before anything else, please let me say with all the sincerity any man ever felt, that I have regretted nothing in my life so much as the inability of Mr. Dreiser and myself to work together amicably in this effort which was so important to us both. I never ceased to hope that he would lose his resentment of me in view of what the Society was accomplishing for Charles Fort's work and fame.

I sympathize with you deeply in your loss, and I hope that you are receiving some solace from the triumph of The Bulwark.[180]

Immediately I knew of Mr. Dreiser's death, I addressed Arthur Leonard Ross, formerly attorney for Mr. Dreiser, asking him how to address you. He said he forwarded my letter to you, but it must have miscarried.

Surely you will agree with me that the place for the Dreiser-Fort correspondence is in the archives of the Fortean Society, which Mr. Dreiser helped to found. If, upon examination, the material appeared to be publishable, we should like to arrange that, with a division of royalties between yourself and the Society.

We could not concur with Mr. Dreiser's attempt to turn over the Fort notes to a university. They would have been buried for all time. Charles Fort fought scholasticism all his life. He willed his notes to *us*, to keep them alive and active. This has been my trust and my responsibility and I have prosecuted it to the best of my ability, at great personal expense in time and money for sixteen years.

I do not know if Mr. Dreiser and you have kept abreast of our progress, but I should be happy to bring you up to date on all details if you wish.

Direct me in what I must do to win from you the confidence Mr. Dreiser never would give me. I hardly need tell you how greatly the Society desires the material you have, how greatly we respect it, how devotedly we should treasure it.

This is ironic. The material Dreiser turned over to the University of Pennsylvania, including the correspondence with Fort, has been freely available to scholars all this time. The material Thayer kept has never been made available to anyone until now. Even its whereabouts were a mystery; it took me a year to track it down and obtain permission for its use.

For a time the Fortean Society had two chapters, one in Chicago and one in San Francisco, in addition to the New York chapter which consisted of Thayer and his friends. In 1949 Thayer grew restive with the activities of these groups and admonished them in the following terms in *Doubt*, number 27:

> Some confusions are arising from the efforts of individual members to organize Forteans who reside in the same locality as themselves into Chapters. The confusions are inherent in the word "organize," which is in itself anathema to nine Forteans out of ten. To the date of writing, the Society might boast, if it wished to, that its membership includes a larger percentage of men and women who "belong" to no other labelled group than any other brotherhood known, among categories less inclusive than the human race or one of the three sexes. It is expressly *because* nobody connected with the Society—and Your Secretary least of all—ever has attempted to "organize" them that these admirably non-joining, flaming individualists do not mind being entered upon our rolls, and welcome the opportunity to make this one exception among societies as such. Indeed we have scores of letters congratulating us upon the achievement of an association which partakes of organizational virtues, but imposes none of the well known penalties.
>
> Probably the Fortean Society is unique in this. At least, YS [Your Secretary, Thayer's

invariable way of referring to himself in *Doubt*] is not aware of any other successfully functioning, ideal anarchy, and it is this eminently Fortean ideal state which suffers when local go-getters attempt to impose commonplace conceptions of organization upon their neighbor-members.

In the heat of enthusiam for the vitality of Fortean philosophy, individuals frequently are inspired to carry The Word to the masses, to meet together and to rally and urge the gentiles to see the Light. An Admirable aim, and every such enthusiast obtains the full cooperation of YS. This is not the only reason men have had for wishing to found Chapters, but is the most usual one, and as long as these local activities do not menace the fame of Charles Fort or the fair name of the Society, even the Smart Apples are encouraged. (By definition, a "Smart Apple" is a Johnny-Come-Lately who thinks he knows a Good Thing when he see it. *Cr* George Ade.)

Unfortunately, the founding of a Chapter is not an unmixed or absolute good. To begin with, in every city where Fortean meetings are held, the members who will NOT attend outnumber those who will by between ten and twenty to one. The non-joining group disparages "lodge meetings," cannot bear the sound of a gavel, refuse to bow to *Robert's Rules of Order* or any other parliamentary procedure or to the will of the majority as expressed by balloting. . . .

The Chapters have no "official" standing whatsoever with the Fortean Society. They are social or study groups, subject only to such rules as they themselves agree to observe. No two Chapters have the same rules, and none of any of their rules stems from Charles Fort, from the Fortean Society or from YS. If fees or local dues are collected, to pay for the hall or for refreshments or for any other purpose, they are disbursed or retained by the Chapter which collects them. No part of such money is ever sent to the Fortean Society. If members are "expelled" from Chapters for non-payment of such dues, or are denied admittance to meetings for any other reason, this does not change their status with the Society. No MFS [Member, Fortean Society] is any less a member for anything a local organizer or locally elected "officer" may say or do. The Fortean Society takes no cognizance of local elections beyond reporting their results as news. The Society does not sponsor any candidates or bless any winners: it does not issue "charters," "authorities," or "privileges": it does not accept responsibility for any speech or action of Chapter "officers." . . .

No prejudice for or against Chapters is to be inferred from the above, and no valid charge of "dictatorship" can be dredged up from it. YS has for 20 years scrupulously avoided handing out any "official" interpretation of Charles Fort, and he has sedulously defended the right of every reader to find in Fort what he will and can. This statement is published here in furtherance of that perfect freedom for all. More specifically, it is published:

1. To inform the entire membership that local Chapters and/or their "officers" have no juris-

> diction over nearby Fortean residents, or over any other members of the Society.
>
> 2. To inform the entire membership that Your Secretary has no wish or inclination to dictate Chapter policies or trends.
> 3. To deny to Chapters and/or their "officers" the right or privilege to publish or utter anything purporting to be an official expression of Forteanism, or to pretend to speak with the voice of the Fortean Society.
> 4. To disclaim responsibility for anything which a Chapter and/or its "officers" may say or do within the Chapter or in dealing with the world outside it. . . .

The San Francisco chapter read this as excommunication, and most of its members resigned. They continued to meet for two years more, still calling themselves "Chapter Two," but not "The Fortean Society." This group was headed by the writer Kenneth MacNicholl, a friend of Thayer's, and had about fifty members. According to Robert Barbour Johnson, Thayer was irritated with the San Francisco members because they were more interested in Fortean phenomena than in "other rebellions" which he considered more important.

> As to the precise cause of the "expulsion," it was, as I remember, the result of an investigation of a collection of alleged "apports" at the Stanford Museum, an article on which appeared in *Fate Magazine.* Fort, of course, was not concerned with "Spiritualist" matters (though he himself conceded that there was a curious resemblance, and possible affinity, between "ap-

> ports" and "teleportations" which were his great discovery, and for which he is perhaps best known to the public). But the curious circumstances under which these were collected (medium enclosed in an iron cage, etc.) convinced some of us that they might well be "teleports." At all events, we decided to examine them, and wrote to the Curator, asking for permission, only to receive the reply that the Museum had no such collection, and never had had! Apart from the *Fate* article, which described it in detail, I myself had seen the collection a few years earlier, and so had several other members. . . . There was quite a bit of correspondence about it, and some of it got reprinted in *Fate*, and Thayer saw it. Whereupon he descended on "Chapter Two" horse, foot and guns![181]

Doubt number 61 was published in the spring of 1959; it was the last. On August 23 Thayer died of a heart attack at the age of fifty-seven.

From the beginning the Fortean Society had been a one-man show. It had no constitution or bylaws and no mechanism for electing any but honorary officers. When Thayer died, no one was able or willing to take his place. Eric Frank Russell, however, points out that the Society was never dissolved and therefore still exists. "The F.S. today is *un*organized, not *dis*organized; there's quite a difference. In fact it may have acquired new members. Every once in a while I get an application to join. Thayer used to accept all such, without quibble, on payment of a couple of bucks. My tactics are different. I mail the application on to the nearest members known to me and leave it to them to handle the newcomer."[182]

Chapter Twelve

One Measures a Circle (1960–1968)

> When a distinguished but elderly scientist states that something is possible, he is almost certainly right. When he states that something is impossible, he is very probably wrong.
>
> Arthur C. Clarke, *Profiles of the Future*

To nearly everybody, somebody else's way of life is an offense. The attitude of orthodox scientists toward Fort is remarkably like that of an Iowa Sunday school teacher toward the beer-drinking, blaspheming town lecher. In Athens they would have given him hemlock.

In a sense, Fort had the best of both worlds; he had the satisfaction of offending orthodoxy with every word he wrote, while at the same time, in his private life, he was able to practice the virtues of simplicity, privacy, and moderation.

The three Fort brothers were taught at the end of a

dog whip that it was necessary to respect authority and to believe what They believed. Raymond learned this lesson as if it were 2+2; Clarence could not learn it, and was cast out; Charles rebelled against it and spent his life in denying it. For twenty-six years he patiently amassed his evidence to prove the innocence of "the damned"—the odd-shaped pieces, rejected and condemned by the puzzle-solvers of science.

If his work disappeared tomorrow, it would be impossible to replace: there are few martyrs, and none for hire.

By and large, Fort has been no luckier in his disciples than any other innovator. A few Fortean writers, like the author of *Mysterious Fires and Lights,* Vincent H. Gaddis, are both able and conscientious. They carry on the work as best they can, and so does a new organization called INFO (International Fortean Organization). Headed by Paul Willis, the organization has some five hundred members here and abroad; it publishes a magazine, *INFO Journal,* which carries valuable studies of Fort's source material as well as original articles on Fortean subjects.

No one who has not tried to write a biography of a man thirty years dead can realize how impossible it is to find out the whole truth. The past is a black hole. Records have vanished, correspondence and photographs have been destroyed, friends and relatives are long dead. The miracle is that it is possible to write of such lives at all.

There are many things I would still like to know: for example, what became of the missing pages of *Many Parts?* Thayer thought the manuscript had been censored, by Fort or someone else, to avoid giving offense to the family. I think this implausible, considering what was left in. Thayer himself, Fort, and Anna, are the only ones who could have censored the manuscript, and it seems unlikely that any of them would have done so. My guess is that Fort cannibalized an early version of the work to make a later one: but where is the later one?

Anna is another mystery. Thayer gives her maiden name as Filan, and later writers have followed him; but on her marriage certificate the name is Filing. Her age is given as twenty-six, meaning that she was born in 1869 or 1870; her parents are identified as John Filing and Catharine Haley of Sheffield. No record of any Anna Filing or Filan born in those years can be found at Somerset House or in the records of the Sheffield Borough Council.

Theresa Fort, Raymond's widow, is still alive; she is ninety-two. The Fort male line is extinct. Neither Charles nor Clarence had any children; Raymond had one daughter. The only collateral descendants that I know of are a grandniece, two great-grandnephews and a great-grandniece, all living in Troy, New York.

Someone who signed herself Harriet Fort had a story in the *New Yorker* in 1962. On a slip of paper attached to the magazine, kept in the Albany Room of the Albany Public Library, someone has written, "Mrs. Hoy H., Saratoga Springs." No such person is known to Mrs. Raymond Fort and her family. I wrote to her in care of the magazine, but had no reply. Perhaps she will read these lines and gratify my curiosity.

Fort's influence on other writers is incalculable; his ideas have diffused so widely that compiling a list of examples would be a hopeless task; I give only a few here.

His "I think we're property" was the inspiration for Eric Frank Russell's novel *Sinister Barrier*, which made its author's reputation among science fiction readers when it was first published serially in 1939. H. Beam Piper's memorable story "He Walked Around the Horses" is taken from Fort's account of the disappearance of Benjamin Bathurst. R. S. Richardson, an American astonomer, writes fiction under the pen name of Philip Latham. As Richardson, he is strictly orthodox and responds with irritation when Fort's name is mentioned; as Latham, he writes Fortean stories.

If I have emphasized the positive qualities of Charles Fort's character, it is because I think them more remarkable than the others. I could have told you that he sometimes quarreled with his wife, that he was sorry for himself on occasion, that he was not always brilliant; but that would have been like announcing that he had two legs.

He practiced the suspension of judgment which many scientists only preach. He wrote:

> I believe nothing of my own that I have ever written. I cannot accept that the products of minds are subject-matter for beliefs.[183]

Over and over again, in a dozen different ways, he emphasized the fluidity of creation, the merging and fading of things into their opposites, the artificiality of all man-made categories. He wrote, "The unadulterated, whether of food we eat, or the air we breathe, or of idealism, or of villainy, is unfindable. Even adultery is adulterated."[184] His books, he said, were fiction, "in the sense that *Pickwick Papers*, and *The Adventures of Sherlock Holmes*, and *Uncle Tom's Cabin;* Newton's *Principia*, Darwin's *Origin of Species*, *Genesis*, *Gulliver's Travels*, and mathematical theorems, and every history of the

United States, and all other histories, are fictions. . . . And yet there is something about the yarns that were told by Dickens that sets them apart, as it were, from the yarns that were told by Euclid. There is much in Dickens' grotesqueries that has the correspondence with experience that is called 'truth,' whereas such Euclidian characters as 'mathematical points' are the vacancies that might be expected from a mind that had had scarcely any experience."[185]

Later he added, "Though I have classed myself with some noted fictionists, I have to accept that the absolute fictionist never has existed. There is a fictional coloration to everybody's account of an 'actual occurrence,' and there is at least the lurk somewhere of what is called the 'actual' in everybody's yarns." He spoke of the often-repeated tales of the man who found a pearl in his oyster stew, the old fiddle that turned out to be a Stradivarius, the lost ring that turned up in a fish's stomach. These are conventional tales, and liars tend to be conventionalists. "But when I come upon the unconventional repeating, in times and places far apart, I feel—even though I have no absolute standards to judge by—that I am outside the field of ordinary liars."[186]

Speaking of poltergeist phenomena, and particularly the falls of stones on rooftops and from appearing-points inside houses, he wrote:

> I point out that these stories of flows of stones are not conventional stories, and are not well known. Their details are not standardized, like "clanking chains" in ghost stories, and "eyes the size of saucers," in sea serpent yarns. Somebody in France, in the year 1842, told of slow-moving stones, and somebody in Sumatra, in the year

> 1903, told of slow-moving stones. It would be strange, if two liars should invent this circumstance—
>
> And that is where I get, when I reason.
>
> If strangeness be a standard for unfavorable judgment, I damn at a swipe most of this book.
>
> But damnation is nothing to me. I offer the data. Suit yourself.[187]

He saw with clarity, more than forty years ago, what others have only begun to suspect in the last decade: that the very categories we think in are suspect, that knowledge cannot be kept in sealed compartments, that the moment we speak of anything as an isolated event, we have already begun to lie.

As Louis Pauwels and Jacques Bergier wrote, in *The Morning of the Magicians:* "Before the first manifestations of Dadaism and Surrealism, Charles Fort introduced into science what Tzara, Breton and their disciples were to introduce into art and literature: a defiant refusal to play at a game where everybody cheats, a furious insistence that there is 'something else.' A huge effort, not so much, perhaps, to grasp reality in its entirety, as to prevent reality being conceived in a falsely coherent way. A rupture that had to be. 'I am a horse-fly that stings the scalp of knowledge to prevent it from sleeping.'"[188]

Fort suspected that the cause-and-effect relationship is an artifact, a consequence of our limited view of the universe; that the truth, if we could know it, would turn out to be much more complicated—not a simple linear series, A, B, C, . . . but a many-dimensioned network. He suspected that events which we consider "real" arrange themselves according to a pattern which has no material existence, like molecules in a forming crystal.

I read this to mean that if all is relation, then stars and men are related, though not by cause and effect. Fossils and strata are there because they are there, because the pattern calls for them to be there; expectations and the results of experiments are related, but not by cause and effect—only as parts of a pattern whose governing principles are continuity, balance, and symmetry.

Fort wrote: "Traceries of ice, millions of years ago, forming on the surface of a pond—later, with different materials, these same forms will express botanically. If something had examined primordial frost, it could have predicted jungles. . . . Mineral specimens now in museums—calcites that are piles of petals—or that long ago were the rough notes of a rose."[189]

He noted that Langley's flying machine appeared a little before the era of aviation, and that Langley could not fly it. "But this machine was capable of flying, because, some years later, Curtis did fly it." One of the greatest of all secrets, he said, "was for ages blabbed by all the pots and kettles in the world," but to no purpose, because it was not yet "steam-engine time."[190]

He may have been wrong about some things, but it is not altogether certain that we can tell which ones they were. His chief crotchet was his insistence that the stars are much nearer than astronomers think. Since the discovery of quasars in 1962 even this seems an open question. Quasars ("quasi-stellar radio sources") have enormous red shifts, and therefore, according to Hubble's law of the expanding universe, must be extremely distant—billions of light-years away. On this assumption, the diameters of some quasars have been measured: they range up to 250,000 light-years. Yet they fluctuate in a period of days. Since nothing can travel faster than the speed of light, this is impossible.

Astronomers are trying to find some other satisfactory way of accounting for the quasars' red shift. I think it is fair to say that if they do not succeed, astronomy will be in a state of crisis..

Fort's vendetta against astronomers often led him into excesses; parts of *New Lands* are embarrassing to read. But at other times, even with the astronomers, he had a lighter touch. In 1926, in a letter to Edmond Hamilton, he wrote: "That big meteor flashed over London, at 9:45 P.M., and, about 9:40 o'clock, I was going down to an underground train. I can't think of any place much more unfavorable for astronomical observations, though perhaps, in another sense, an Observatory is."[191]

It was the gentleness of his irony that made it so devastating. Unlike Thayer, he was an essentially modest man who considered all human beings absurd, including himself. Somehow he had found the balance and self-effacement that Eastern mystics strive for; he would have made a good Zen Buddhist.

In the thirty-six years since his death, Fort's harvest of oddities has gone right on falling from the sky. On June 7, 1937, for example, the streamline train *City of Denver* arrived in Chicago with its headlamp broken. Inside the broken lamp was a dead trout.[192] In October, 1944, a live golden trout was found in soot cleaned from a chimney by Mrs. Dorothy Banner in Bournemouth, England.[193] On the night of October 11, 1949, a Mrs. Walker, of Bristol, England, was awakened by a noise; she found a goldfish flopping in her fireplace.[194]

Frogs rained from the sky in Tarpa, Hungary, Decatur, Illinois, and Batavia, New York, all between August and October, 1937.[195] On August 14, 1948, on a day of thick mist, frogs fell on Towyn, Merionethshire, Wales, so copiously that "brooms and shovels could hardly keep them out of houses." On June 24, 1944, thousands of live perch, two and a half to four inches long, were found in puddles left by a rainstorm on a farm near Hillsdale, Michigan.[196]

Red rain fell in the region of Fontanella, near Bergamo, Italy, in April, 1942.[197] Green rain, Dayton, Ohio, in March, 1948,[198] and in Mobile, Alabama, in July, 1948.[199] Gray snow fell on Basle, Switzerland, February 7, 1942;[200] black snow on parts of Bulgaria in March, 1944;[201] vari-colored snow near Hancock, New Hampshire, on March 2, 1948—first yellow, then pink, then purple.[202] In July, 1968, red, orange, gray, and yellow mud fell on southern England, splattering cars and pedestrians.[203]

Conventionalists continue to ignore these events, or explain them away. But Fort has made it impossible for us to turn our backs forever; his laughter, like the trumpets of Jericho, has left cracks in the wall of orthodoxy, and they are spreading. He did not hope to succeed in capturing reality entire, but he did remind us, so trenchantly that we can never forget, that it is necessary to try.

When *Lo!* was set in proofs, Sussman showed him a page that was one line short. The passage ended: "But, if there is an underlying oneness of all things, it does not matter where we begin, whether with stars, or laws of supply and demand, or frogs, or Napoleon Bonaparte."

Without hesitation, Fort picked up a pencil and wrote: "One measures a circle, beginning anywhere."[204]

Notes

Charles Fort wrote and published five books in his lifetime. One was a novel, *The Outcast Manufacturers* (B. W. Dodge, 1909). The other four, *The Book of the Damned, Lo!, New Lands,* and *Wild Talents,* were reprinted in an omnibus volume, *The Books of Charles Fort* (Holt, 1941), with an introduction by Tiffany Thayer and an index by Henry Schlanger.

A number of brief articles and essays about Fort have appeared in books and periodicals, but the only one of these which contains new material of value is Miriam Allen deFord's "Charles Fort: Enfant Terrible of Science." Fort was an intensely private person, and even his confidants, Thayer and Dreiser, did not know much about his early life. For this, Fort's unpublished manuscript, *Many Parts,* is almost the only source.

CHAPTER ONE

1 Founded in this country by one Jan Fort, otherwise Vandervort, La Fort, or Van Fort, also known as Jan Libbertee, whose marriage in New Amsterdam was recorded in 1641.

2 August 6, 1874.

3 For this and other personal reminiscences of the Fort family I am indebted to Mrs. Raymond Fort.

4 *Many Parts,* 23–24. Unless otherwise noted, these page numbers are from a manuscript retyped by Tiffany Thayer, probably some time

in the thirties, as part of Thayer's projected biography of Fort. The typescript begins with a brief introduction, "The Forts of Albany," and includes some speculations by Thayer, mostly erroneous, about the events and personages of *Many Parts.* In addition to the typescript, Thayer left hundreds of pages handwritten in pencil on yellow paper, but Fort is barely mentioned in them: they are all about Tiffany Thayer.

5 *MP,* 25.
6 *MP,* 25–26.
7 *MP,* 35.
8 *MP,* 37.
9 *MP,* 34–35.
10 *MP,* 43. (Page 82 in Fort's original typescript.)
11 *MP,* 33–34.
12 *MP,* 55.
13 *MP,* 56.
14 *MP,* 53.
15 *MP,* 60–61.
16 *MP,* 46–47.
17 *MP,* 75.
18 *MP,* 39.
19 *MP,* 40.
20 *MP,* 52.
21 *MP,* 36.
22 *MP,* 67–68.
23 *MP,* 72.
24 *MP,* 80–81.
25 *MP,* 83–84.
26 Mrs. Raymond Fort.
27 *MP,* 84–85.
28 John S. Hoy, then in the plumbing business like his father, had worked as a reporter for the *World* in his youth. See Albany *Times Union,* April 20, 1922.
29 *MP,* 89.
30 Fort kept this curious ability, and used it many years later to record the conversation of "queer boarding house people."
31 *MP,* 105.

CHAPTER TWO

32 Mrs. Raymond Fort.
33 *The Outcast Manufacturers.*
34 Mrs. Raymond Fort.
35 Unpublished transcript of Theodore Dreiser's interview with Anna Fort, September 1933, recorded by Dreiser's secretary, Evelyn Light.
36 Mrs. Raymond Fort.
37 *The Books of Charles Fort,* xx.
38 In one of them (March 5, 1901) he wrote, "I have just returned

from the hospital where I learned that at least the dread and uncertainty are over. I don't remember much about walking up, my suspense and fears were so great and I don't know down which avenue I returned. . . ."

39 Unpublished journal, entry of February 25 [1908]: "Things just as bad, nothing yet sold, but I have hopes from Collier's and Harpers —only the good old hope without backing, because stories kept longer than usual. Can't go out without getting feet soaking, because poor shoes. Everything just as miserable and horrible as ever—oh, hell! It's good for me! Nothing like it to develop this poor damn fool who thinks he's a genius."

40 *Tom Watson's Magazine,* 1906.

41 "Ructions," *TWM,* May 1906.

42 Memoir by Theodore Dreiser, published after his death in *My Life With Dreiser,* by Helen Dreiser, 220.

43 *The Books of Charles Fort, xvii.*

44 *The Outcast Manufacturers,* 301–2.

45 See note 41.

46 *Popular Magazine,* September 1905.

47 *The Books of Charles Fort, xvii.*

48 Anthony Boucher, in an afterword to Miriam Allen deFord's essay, "Charles Fort: Enfant Terrible of Science," *The Magazine of Fantasy and Science Fiction,* January 1954.

49 *The Outcast Manufacturers,* 94.

50 *OM,* 28–29.

51 See note 48.

52 *OM,* 4.

53 *OM,* 13.

54 *OM,* 15.

55 *OM,* 101.

56 *OM,* 75.

57 *OM,* 256.

58 *OM,* 300.

59 *OM,* 261.

CHAPTER THREE

60 *The Books of Charles Fort, xix–xx.*

61 *BCF,* 975.

62 Letter dated "Dec. 1 '19," but internal evidence makes it clear that this is an error for 1915.

63 *BCF, xix.*

64 *The Symmes' Theory of Concentric Spheres* (1878) sets forth the theories of Americus Symmes's father, Captain John Cleves Symmes of the United States Infantry, who spent the last ten years of his life trying to convince the public that the Earth is made up of five concentric hollow spheres, with openings a thousand miles wide at the poles. In 1822 and 1823 he petitioned Congress to finance an expedition to discover the north polar opening.

65 *Our Inheritance in the Great Pyramid* (1864). Smyth, the Astronomer-Royal of Scotland, believed that by measuring the internal passageways of the Great Pyramid in "Pyramid inches," a record of past and future history can be disclosed: markings in the passageways indicate the creation of the world (A.D. 4004), the Flood, the Exodus, and so on. The record stops at a point somewhere between 1882 and 1911, indicating the end of the world.
66 See note 62. Cf. W. A. Swanberg, *Dreiser,* 231.
67 Fort to Dreiser, March 31, 1916.
68 Fort to Dreiser, June 3, 1916.
69 *My Life With Dreiser,* 222–23. See note 42.
70 Fort to Dreiser, January 21, 1918. Part of this letter is misquoted in *Dreiser,* 269. Swanberg could not cope with Fort's handwriting; the best he could make of this was "The sensation of enclosing an organism is delightfully revolting."

CHAPTER FOUR

71 *The Books of Charles Fort,* 1026.
72 *BCF,* 850.
73 *BCF,* 918.
74 *BCF,* 544.
75 *BCF,* 547–48.
76 *BCF,* 23.
77 *BCF,* 548.
78 *BCF,* 758.
79 *BCF,* 3–4.
80 Reprinted in *The Fortean Society Magazine,* number 2, October 1937.
81 Reprinted in *FSM,* number 3, January 1940.
82 *BCF,* 17.
83 *BCF,* 111.
84 *BCF,* 545.
85 *BCF,* 546.
86 *BCF,* 40–41.
87 *The Atmosphere,* 402–3.
88 A, 406–7.
89 A, 412–14.
90 *BCF,* 255–56.
91 *BCF,* 90–91.
92 *BCF,* 33.

CHAPTER FIVE

93 *The Books of Charles Fort,* 751–52.
94 *BCF,* 18.
95 *BCF,* 16.

96 *BCF*, 234.
97 *BCF*, 270–71.
98 *BCF*, 168.
99 *BCF*, 853–54.

CHAPTER SIX

100 *The Planet Venus*, 95.
101 *PV*, 96.
102 *PV*, 92–93.
103 *The Books of Charles Fort*, 525.
104 *BCF*, 199.
105 R. A. Proctor, *Old and New Astronomy*, 651.
106 Willy Ley, *Mariner IV to Mars*, 73.
107 *Old and New Astronomy*, 123.
108 Data tables for the years 1966 and 1967 cannot be used for statistical purposes because they include a "Pending" category.
109 *UFOs—Identified*, 171.
110 Cf. *Scientific Study of Unidentified Flying Objects*, sometimes called the Condon Report. This is commonly regarded as an anti-UFO document, an impression justified by the introduction written by Dr. Edward U. Condon. The text itself, however, discusses in detail a number of investigated cases in which the testimony of witnesses could neither be explained nor dismissed. One of the most striking of these is Case 2, involving multiple visual-radar sightings in Greenwich, Connecticut, in 1956, of which the authors say bluntly: "In conclusion, although conventional or natural explanations certainly cannot be ruled out, the probability of such seems low in this case and the probability that at least one genuine UFO was involved appears to be fairly high."
111 *The Books of Charles Fort*, 283.
112 *BCF*, 293.
113 *BCF*, 292. If this had occurred during the present decade, it would surely have been put down as debris from a space shot or a decaying satellite. Compare the following report of a sighting in Indiana on March 3, 1968 (New York *Times*, July 2, 1968): "'It was at about treetop level and was seen very very clearly and was just a few yards away. . . . All of the observers saw a long jet airplane looking vehicle without any wings. It was on fire both in front and behind. All observers also saw many windows in the U.F.O.'" The Air Force explained this as "the re-entry into the atmosphere of the booster rocket, or other launching components, of Zond 4, a space vehicle launched from the Soviet Union the day before." And that's fine for 1968, but what about 1907—whose booster rocket was that?
114 *BCF*, 513.
115 *BCF*, 296–97.
116 *BCF*, 517.

117 *BCF*, 516.
118 *BCF*, 279.

CHAPTER SEVEN

119 Michel Gauquelin, *The Cosmic Clocks*, 188.
120 *The Books of Charles Fort*, 598.
121 *BCF*, 679.
122 *Encyclopaedia Britannica*, article "Lemmings."
123 Leonard W. Wing, "Time Chart Measurements of Norwegian Lemming and Rodent Cycles," *Journal of Cycle Research*, January 1957.
124 *BCF*, 742–47.
125 *BCF*, 738–39.
126 *BCF*, 953.

CHAPTER EIGHT

127 *The Structure of Scientific Revolutions*, x.
128 *SSR*, 149.
129 *Old and New Astronomy*, 570.
130 *SSR*, 77.
131 *SSR*, 64.
132 *SSR*, 143.
133 See James D. Watson, *The Double Helix*.
134 *SSR*, 133–34.
135 For many details, see Alfred de Grazia, ed., *The Velikovsky Affair*.
136 *Harper's*, December 1963.
137 *Science*, December 21, 1962.
138 *Harper's*, June 1951.
139 See page 133.
140 *Nature*, May 14, 1960.
141 Ralph E. Juergens, in *The Velikovsky Affair*, 52–53.
142 *VA*, 94.
143 *VA*, 95.
144 *The Books of Charles Fort*, 53.
145 *BCF*, 479.
146 *BCF*, 481–82.
147 *BCF*, 571.
148 *Old* and *New Astronomy*, 651.
149 *The New Intelligent Man's Guide to Science*, 311.

CHAPTER NINE

150 In Damon Knight, ed., *The Shape of Things*.
151 Dennis Rawlins, "The Mysterious Case of the Planet Pluto," *Sky and Telescope*, March 1968.

152 *Man and Time,* 225–27.
153 *October the First Is Too Late,* 64. Page numbers from the Fawcett paperback edition.
154 *OFITL,* 68.
155 *Many Parts,* 68.

CHAPTER TEN

156 Fort to Dreiser, November 7, 1920.
157 Dreiser interview with Anna Fort.
158 Fort to Raymond Fort and family, January 12, 1921.
159 See *The Books of Charles Fort,* 534.
160 Miriam Allen deFord, "Charles Fort, Enfant Terrible of Science," *The Magazine of Fantasy and Science Fiction,* January 1954. (See note 48.) Anthony Boucher, then the editor of *Fantasy and Science Fiction,* added this footnote: "My own first meeting with Miss deFord came about when I investigated a similar stone-fall case in Oakland, California, in 1943. We compared notes and found our experiences almost identical—save that in 1943 there was no Fort to whom to report the details; and as a result the Oakland case will be known to future researchers only in the misleading and sometimes outright mendacious reports of the daily press."
161 *Weird Tales,* August 1931.
162 *Science and Invention,* April 1926.
163 Fort to Hamilton, May 27, 1926.
164 Hamilton to Knight, December 29, 1967.
165 Fort to Hamilton, October 25, 1926.
166 *The Books of Charles Fort,* 976–80.
167 Fort to Hamilton, February 17, 1931.
168 Thayer to Fort, August 20, 1930.
169 *BCF, xvi.*
170 *BCF, xx.* See also *BCF,* 62.
171 Dreiser interview with Anna Fort.
172 Fort to Dreiser, November 19, 1930.
173 Fort to Shipley, March 1, 1931.
174 The bulk of these notes are in the Thayer Collection of the New York Public Library (an estimated 60,000 of them), but the notes recording Fort's last illness were kept by Aaron Sussman for Mrs. Thayer and are still in his possession. All the notes are on curious oblong bits of paper, irregular in shape and not uniform in size; some are about 1½"×2½", some a little larger. The paper is pinkish and coarse, more like cheap wrapping paper than anything else. It looks as if Fort had a lifetime supply of this stuff, and tore off scraps (against a ruler, maybe) a few at a time as he needed them.
175 The death certificate reads, in part: "I hereby certify that the foregoing particulars . . . are correct as near as the same can be ascertained, and I further certify that deceased was admitted to this institu-

tion on May 2, 1932, that I last saw him alive on the 3 day of May, 1932, that he died on the 3 day of May 1932, about 11:55 o'clock A.M., and that I am unable to state definitely the cause of death; the diagnosis during his last illness was: Cardiac Failure, dilatation, duration 15 ds. Contributory, splenomyologenous leukemia, duration 2 yrs." All this is little more than an elaborate confession of ignorance. "Dilatation" is enlargement of the heart. "Splenomyologenous" means originating in the spleen and bone marrow. Since the doctor who signed this certificate saw Fort for the first time on May 2, the day he was admitted to the hospital, his diagnosis of splenomyologenous leukemia sounds like nothing but a translation into ritual language of Anna's testimony (see the Dreiser interview) that she had begged Fort not to drink so much lemonade, grapefruit juice, ginger ale—"all that sour stuff," because it would "dry up his blood." As far as I can determine, no autopsy was performed, and the real cause of Fort's death is unknown.

CHAPTER ELEVEN

176 Thayer to Dreiser, March 11, 1935.
177 Dreiser to Thayer, March 16, 1935.
178 See chapter nine.
179 Russell to Knight, April 24, 1967.
180 Dreiser's posthumous novel. It was coolly received by the critics, but sold very well.
181 Johnson to Knight, February 1968.
182 See note 179.

CHAPTER TWELVE

183 *The Books of Charles Fort,* 555–56.
184 *BCF,* 1061
185 *BCF,* 863.
186 *BCF,* 864.
187 *BCF,* 566.
188 *The Morning of the Magicians,* 147 (Avon paperback edition). This is a double mistranslation from Miriam Allen deFord's essay quoted in chapter ten. The French has *"le cuir,"* meaning the hide, but in the translation to English again it becomes the scalp.
189 *BCF,* 542.
190 *BCF,* 530.
191 Fort to Hamilton, October 25, 1926. A portion of this letter is quoted in chapter ten.
192 *The Fortean Society Magazine,* number 1. It was explained that the train had hit an eagle with a fish in its mouth.
193 *Time,* October 9, 1944.
194 *Doubt,* number 27.

195 *FSM,* number 3.
196 *Doubt,* number 20.
197 *FSM,* number 9.
198 *Doubt,* number 21.
199 *Doubt,* number 23.
200 *FSM,* number 7.
201 *Doubt,* number 11.
202 Boston *Globe,* March 2, 1948.
203 New York *Times,* July 2, 1968. The mud fell during a heat wave, on the hottest day in seven years. The Weather Bureau said it was dust and sand, "drawn up by storms" from the Sahara and southern Spain.
204 *The Books of Charles Fort,* 544.

INDEX